the Art of
LEADERSHIP

DEVELOPING PEOPLE
IN EARLY CHILDHOOD ORGANIZATIONS

Exchange Press

7700 A Street

Lincoln, Nebraska 68510

(800) 221-2864 • ExchangePress.com

the Art of LEADERSHIP

Developing People in Early Childhood Organizations

The Art of Leadership series replaces the popular Exchange Press textbook, *The Art of Leadership: Managing Early Childhood Organizations.* The entire series demonstrates the great complexity of an early childhood leader's job. Each volume expresses the importance of one aspect of this role. Each leader will need to prioritize all these roles based on many factors, including the skills that reside within the members of his team.

These articles were originally published in *Exchange* magazine. Every attempt has been made to update information on authors and other contributors to these articles. We apologize for any biographical information that is not current. *Exchange* is a bimonthly management magazine for directors, owners, and teachers of early childhood programs. For more information about *Exchange* and other Exchange Press publications for directors and teachers, contact:

Exchange Press
7700 A Street
Lincoln, Nebraska 68510
(800) 221-2864 • ExchangePress.com

ISBN 978-0-942702-60-6

Printed by Thomson-Shore Inc. in Dexter, Michigan

© Exchange Press, 2019

Cover Design: Scott Bilstad

the Art of
LEADERSHIP

DEVELOPING PEOPLE
IN EARLY CHILDHOOD ORGANIZATIONS

Introduction

On Teaching *by Lilian G. Katz* 7

Chapter 1: Selecting Staff

Caregivers of Quality *by Sally Cartwright* 12

Hiring for Professional, Creative Imagination *by Ian Broinowski* 15

Interviewing: A Pedagogical Approach *by Anne Marie Coughlin* 20

Questions that Get You Great Teachers *by Jennifer Carsen* 24

Observing Teaching Candidates in Action *by Roger Neugebauer* 28

Hiring and Retaining Male Staff *by Bruce Cunningham* 33

Bringing Diversity into Your Center *by Thomas Moore* 38

Chapter 2: Training Staff

Helping Adults Succeed *by Gigi Schweikert* 44

Intentional and Embedded Professional Development *by Sandra Duncan* 48

Creating Environments Where Teachers, Like Children,
Learn Through Play *by Elizabeth Jones* 53

Creative Staff Training is Key to Quality *by Karen Stephens* 58

Principles and Strategies for Coaching and Mentoring *by Margie Carter* 63

Mentors as Teachers, Learners, and Leaders *by Marcy Whitebook and Dan Bellm* 69

The Spirit of Adult Play *by Bonnie Neugebauer* 75

Chapter 3: Appraising Staff

Performance Appraisals: One Step in a Comprehensive
Staff Supervision Model *by Susan Kilbourne.* 78

Monitoring, Measuring, and Evaluating Staff Performance *by Kay M. Albrecht* 83

Guidelines for Effective Use of Feedback *by Roger Neugebauer* 87

Looking Inside: Helping Teachers Assess Their Beliefs and Values *by Paula Jorde Bloom* 91

Evaluating Staff Performance: A Valuable Training Tool *by Margie Carter* 94

Overcome the Fear of Firing *by Roger Neugebauer* 97

Chapter 4: Promoting Teamwork

All the Teachers are Friends Here *by Nancy Rosenow* 104

Ten Strategies for Coaching a Winning Team *by Pam Schiller* 108

Step-by-Step Guide to Team Building *by Roger Neugebauer* 112

Using the Rules of Improvisation to Build Playful Teams *by Kelly Matthews* 119

Learning to Play Well with Others *by Jeny Searcy* 125

Indicators of Effective Teamwork *by Margie Carter* 129

When Friction Flares: Dealing with Staff Conflict *by Roger Neugebauer* 134

Ten Teamwork Terminators and Some Cures *by Hawaii Directors Network attendees* 139

On Teaching

by Lilian G. Katz

From time to time it is a good idea for those of us who teach to take a look at ourselves as teachers and to reflect on our own roles. On the basis of my reflections, I want to share 14 points that you may find useful in your teaching.

1

Teaching involves many conflicting pressures and situations. We cannot respond fully or equally to all of them. We have to decide what is worth making an issue over. Don't have too many issues. A half dozen will do! Take your stand on these issues with clarity and courage — for the sake of the children.

2

Teaching requires constant decision making. And every decision carries with it its own potential for error. There are no error-free decisions. For example, if we decide to screen young children with tests, we will make many errors; the younger the children, the more likely we are to make the error of mislabeling them.

If we don't screen and test children, we may make the error of failing to identify those children who can

be greatly helped by early intervention. Either way, we will make errors. We have to decide which is the least worst error. Thus, teaching involves a series of choices of which errors we prefer.

3

In teaching, all we have at a given moment, in a given situation, is our own best judgment. Throughout our lives, we study and reflect in order to refine that judgment; we talk with colleagues, examine our own efforts — all in order to improve our judgment. In the last analysis, our best judgment is all there is.

4

It is important to strive for a balance between having sufficient skepticism to go on learning and sufficient conviction to go on acting — for to teach is to act, and effective teaching requires action with optimum confidence in the rightness of what we are doing.

5

We must cultivate our own intellect and nourish the life of the mind. For teachers, the cultivation of the mind is as important as the cultivation of understanding and compassion.

6

We should take others' views seriously, for we may learn from them. But we should never take others' views more seriously than we take our own, for that is the essence of self-respect, and children need to be taught by self-respecting adults.

7

We must each see ourselves as developing professionals. That is, we must become lifelong students of our own teaching.

8

It is a good idea to respect our adversaries and resist the temptation to be defensive toward them. Remember, whenever we respond defensively it is partly because we believe the attack, or at least part of it. Thus we are responding according to the attacker's rules.

Remember also that adversaries and enemies tend to become alike!

9

It is helpful to assume that the people we work with have the capacities for greatness, creativity, courage, and insight. Occasionally, this assumption will be wrong. But if we always make it, we will be much more likely to uncover and support these capacities in others.

10

Never underestimate the power of ideas — bad ones as well as good ones! Ideas are distinctly human creations, and if they were not powerful, many people would not have been imprisoned, exiled, and executed for them. In our own times, we have seen the power of ideas of Mahatma Gandhi and Martin Luther King, and are seeing today the power of the idea of democracy in China.

11

We cannot have optimum environments for children in schools unless the environments are also optimum for adults who work with those children. Certainly, on some days what is optimum for the children is obtained at the expense of the adults, and vice versa on other days. But on an average day-to-day basis, both children and adults must find their lives together satisfying and interesting.

12

Almost every semester, I ask a university class of 30 to 35 graduate students how many of them feel that a teacher has made a significant difference in their lives. Invariably there will be two or three who reveal that a single teacher, by showing concern or encouragement, saved their psychological lives. Just think how many children that adds up to over a career that involves teaching 30 or 35 children a year for 25 or 30 years — it could be more than 100 people. That's a lot of lives to make a real difference to!

13

Teachers have a major role to play in the struggle for equality. But for what equality are we struggling? We are not equally tall or musical or athletic or beautiful. But we are equally human! We are equally human in that we all have hopes and dreams, and fears and doubts. We all want to feel loved by someone, to be treated with respect and dignity. In these ways, all of the world's people have much more in common than they have apart!

14

I really believe that each of us must come to care about everyone else's children. We must come to see that the welfare of our children and grandchildren is intimately linked to the welfare of all other people's children. After all, when one of our children needs life-saving surgery, someone else's child will perform it. If one of our children is threatened or harmed by violence, someone else's child will be responsible for the violent act. The good life for our own children can only be secured if a good life is also secured for all other people's children. Where are other people's children right now? Are they having wholesome, caring, and appropriate experiences? The person who will be our president 60 years from now may be in someone's three-year-old class today. I hope she is having a good experience! To be concerned about other people's children is not just a practical matter — it is a moral and ethical one.

Adapted and reprinted from *ERIC EECE Newsletter*, Summer 1989, with permission of ERIC Clearinghouse on Elementary and Early Childhood Education, University of Illinois at Urbana-Champaign, 805 West Pennsylvania Avenue, Urbana, IL 61801.

Lilian G. Katz

Lilian G. Katz, PhD, Professor Emerita, University of Illinois, Urbana-Champaign, is Co-Director of the Clearinghouse on Early Education and Parenting and Editor of *Early Childhood Education and Parenting*.

the *Art of*
LEADERSHIP

DEVELOPING PEOPLE
IN EARLY CHILDHOOD ORGANIZATIONS

CHAPTER 1

Selecting Staff

Caregivers of Quality *by Sally Cartwright* 12

Hiring for Professional, Creative Imagination *by Ian Broinowski* 15

Interviewing: A Pedagogical Approach *by Anne Marie Coughlin* 20

Questions that Get You Great Teachers *by Jennifer Carsen* 24

Observing Teaching Candidates in Action *by Roger Neugebauer* 28

Hiring and Retaining Male Staff *by Bruce Cunningham* 33

Bringing Diversity into Your Center *by Thomas Moore* 38

Caregivers of Quality

by Sally Cartwright

Building toward a top-notch child care staff is anything but easy. More than love for children, more than training and experience makes a valuable caregiver. Below, named in bold type, are the essential ingredients in caregivers of quality.

Good physical health is a prerequisite for caregivers at work with young children. More difficult to assess is **emotional maturity**. It was clarified by Barbara Biber of Bank Street College of Education when she wrote that a caregiver "needs to be a person so secure within herself that she can function with principles rather than prescriptions, that she can exert authority without requiring submission, that she can work experimentally but not at random, and that she can admit mistakes without feeling humiliated" (Barbara Biber, in *Childhood Education*, March 1948).

One discerns such qualities in a caregiver neither by résumé nor interview, but by observing him at work with children. Watch the caregiver for these qualities, and watch the children as well, for their behavior reflects caregiver competence. Is there cooperative child initiative? Is there a mix of friendly humor and purpose? Most of all, are the children deeply involved in their work and play? Clear, consistent evidence of a caregiver's personal integration and inner sense of security is truly important for his success with children.

A matured and perceptive **kindness** or unconditional love, so important in good caregivers, means both heart and detachment (discussed below) in helping children to help themselves. A good caregiver knows intuitively what child at which moment requires warm and close concern. She is approachable and friendly. She listens well, gives support as needed, and shares in laughter with, not at, the children. A good caregiver is keenly aware of emotional and physical safety for each child. His care is shown in constructing the environment for active child learning with his discerning choice of equipment, materials, and spatial arrangement within a consistent, predictable program framework. Children need the support of steady, warm approval. A good caregiver may condemn a child's words or action, but not the child himself.

A good caregiver needs courage and integrity. **Courage** means a strong, upbeat will to work through whatever odds for what one most cares about, in this case the children. A courageous caregiver goes to bat for child needs, often working closely with other staff members, parents, and/or community leaders.

Integrity means a well-knit personality along with honesty in all one does. It means what Polonius told his son: "To thine own self be true, and it must follow as the night the day, thou canst not then be false to any man" (Shakespeare).

As caregivers develop **self-awareness**, they improve each quality mentioned as well as self-evaluation. Caregivers may help each other toward self-awareness through constructive criticism with mutual trust and respect. Quiet reflection and professional counseling may help as well. Working with children will sometimes stir emotions from the caregiver's own childhood. A truly fine caregiver will have searched and brought to light salient unconscious factors in herself. She's aware of their influence when at work with children, and steers her own behavior accordingly.

Good caregivers need a **theoretical ground**, a conceptual framework in which to see children. The developmental-interaction point of view put forward by Bank Street College of Education (Betty Boegehold, Harriet Cuffaro, William Hooks, and Gordon Klopf, *Education Before Five*, Bank Street College, 1977; Barbara Biber, Ellen Shapiro, and Elaine Wickens, *Promoting Cognitive Growth from a Developmental-Interaction Point of View*, NAEYC, 1971; and Ellen Shapiro and Barbara Biber, *The Education of Young Children: A Developmental-Interaction Approach*, Teachers College Record, Vol. 74, No. 1, September 1972) is perhaps the most useful foundation and guide for helping youngsters learn at their best. The word 'development' suggests a continuing, complex process of growth and learning, while interaction occurs internally between the child's emotional, physical, and cognitive growth, and externally between the child and his expanding physical and social environment. The accent is on integrative action by the children themselves. Developmental-interaction is clearly aligned with NAEYC's developmentally appropriate practice (Sue Bredekamp & C. Copple, *Developmentally Appropriate Practice in Early Childhood Programs*, NAEYC, 1997).

Research in the last ten years indicates that a caregiver's intellectual understanding of DAP is often sadly unable to implement appropriate practice with the children (Loraine Dunn and Susan Kontos, "What Have We Learned About Developmentally Appropriate Practice?," *Young Children*, July 1997). Hands-on workshops can be somewhat helpful in training caregivers, but protracted, daily participant experience in a child care environment that supports active child learning, peer cooperation, creativity, and the keen interest shared by the children in their self-impelled work of learning together is by all odds the best training for beginning caregivers.

A good caregiver, daily responsible for child experience, should have, besides the thorough background in developmental psychology mentioned above, the **equivalent of a college graduate's general knowledge**, and effective access to the media, libraries, and the Internet. Experience with elemental care of our physical environment and with young children's books is also valuable, while a working knowledge of grassroots democracy will support cooperative learning. It is through cooperative learning experience from age three onward that children gradually come to understand the benefits and responsibilities of democratic community, which, not incidentally, is so important to the health of our country today.

Child care experts know that, aside from their attainment of needed skills, young children do not need proficiency in traditional academic subjects. The salient point is not so much what, but how, they learn. And, again, how children learn best is through their own action: asking questions, finding answers, and testing their answers by using them in their work and play, all with adult guidance, not didactic instruction. Good caregivers know the value of a child's innate curiosity and deep satisfaction in the experiential learning process. Let no child care environment dampen a child's interest and joy in learning!

Good caregivers show unfailing **warm respect for and courtesy to children** as a group and to each child as a unique and unrepeatable individual. Helping a child to make constructive, independent choices toward self-disciplined creativity depends very much upon our genuine, full, and caring respect for that child and his way of working, his way of learning. Such respect cannot be accomplished without a very real knowledge of child development, as well as the personal caregiver qualities of inner security, integrity, and self-awareness.

Allied to respect is a good caregiver's **trust in each child** to find his own way, in a supportive child care environment, toward personal integrity, acceptable behavior, good learning purpose, and ultimately to realize his unique potential. Genuine trust in a child depends on fundamental knowledge of child development, close observation of the individual child, and the caregiver's own inner sense of security mentioned above.

Integrity and respect invite **discretion**. A child's problems should remain confidential. Respect for the privacy of the child and her family is essential for their trust and confidence in the caregiver.

Contrary to strictly linear thinking, which western science and philosophy have championed for three centuries, **intuition**, a non-reasoning, often quite sudden insight is finally gaining credence. Einstein said, "Imagination is more important than knowledge," and imagination lives with intuition. For many of us, intuition often sways our thinking simply because it feels right and it works. A well-balanced, mature, and keenly observant caregiver knows in her bones how to be with a child.

Professional **detachment** allows respect, trust, and kindness (unconditional love) to come through to the child. On the surface, detachment and love may seem a paradox, but precisely the opposite is true. A caregiver with inner security and mature self-awareness, a caregiver at ease and fulfilled by her own adult development, does not impose her personality needs onto her relations with children.

Detachment in caring allows empathy without projection, without naively attributing her own unconscious negative feelings to the children. Detachment gives the children psychological space. It avoids sarcasm and contempt, which are crushing to a child. Detachment helps the caregiver test and use her knowledge of child development with a degree of wisdom.

Don't forget **laughter**. One sign of detachment is often delightful humor, and humor in the classroom is important. It signals enjoyment. It invites friendship. It often opens the way for cooperative learning. While shared humor lights the morning, laughing at a child's expense should be nipped at once. Affectionate laughter is an indispensable quality in good child care.

Finally, the **caregiver is a model**. Whether conscious of it or not, he models feeling, thought, and behavior for the children in his care. An inevitable part of child learning is copying; trying to think, feel, and act like persons consistently near and admired by the child. A beloved provider may demonstrate values which the children cherish all their lives. The personality of a caregiver, her instinctive kindness, her deep integrity, her lively interest in life and learning, will all affect the children. It is a sobering responsibility, an inspiring challenge.

Sally Cartwright

Sally Cartwright, with a BA from Cornell and MS from Bank Street College of Education, has worked over 50 years in the field of education as teacher, administrator, consultant, and author. Her thrust has been to understand the finest possible learning toward the goals of a rewarding adulthood and responsible, democratic citizenship. She has taught all ages from mature teachers and university students down to three year olds, whose experiential learning, she says, is especially valuable for their later years in school, college, and beyond. She has authored eight books for children and numerous articles on education.

Hiring for Professional, Creative Imagination

by Ian Broinowski

The room was vibrant. The children were engrossed; Julie was enchanting as an educator. I was observing Julie and her children making a dinosaur as part of my Ph.D study in a small center in Brisbane, Australia. I was simply entranced by her work. There was a buzz of activity — learning and life going on as I sat enthralled by her almost magical and certainly inspirational involvement with her children and their learning. It was one of those moments we all cherish in our work as teachers — a time we just want to hang onto forever — the smell of glue, the chatter, the creativity, the mess, and the smiles and laughter. All this combined to make something unique, special, and simply beautiful.

At another center, I felt a sense of dismay as I observed an all too familiar table of organized collage and paints being prepared by the staff. They were all caring, well-trained educators with a collective wealth of experience, but their work with children was mediocre.

These two cases illustrate my dilemma and has lead me to pursue a constant and perplexing question over the last decade or so. My struggle has been to find out what makes some educators quite simply outstanding in their work. What makes the difference between the two examples above? Why do I inwardly smile when I enter one program with an overwhelming sense of "Oh, wow!" and sigh in the other?

To answer this question I have drawn from the world of art, music, and drama to examine the fundamental notion that perhaps working with young children is in fact more of an art form than a science. This view led me to seriously challenge the almost obsessive reliance on scientific methodology in our study of children.

But why was it so unusual? The same scene is played out in early childhood programs all over the world every day. Children and their teachers are intertwined as they explore a myriad of activities together. And yet my experience has been that really creative, imaginative, and enchanting programs for young children are the exception.

Just as there are exceptional artists, musicians, writers, and sculptors, I wanted to find out what it is about exceptional educators and why they are different.

Artists are in some sense enchanted by their work. They, like early childhood educators are delighted, fascinated, and utterly captivated by their work. Artists are charmed by light, colour, shading, and visual expression. An educator, too, is charmed by children, their relationships, and their own incredulity of life.

I also wanted to explore imagination. To imagine is to be human. An artist and an educator both produce ideas; they create mental images of what does not exist, or things they have yet to experience. Imagination is a powerful force in our lives. It has created greatness and great sadness in human history. But all our historical figures in education have possessed powerful imagination. Eventually my quest lead me to wonder what role professional creativity plays in our work with young children.

Professional Creativity and Program Quality

My examination of these issues did indeed indicate that there is a relationship between an early childhood educator's sense of enchantment, imagination, and creativity and their work with young children. There is a clear correlation between an educator's professional creative imagination and the creativeness of the children in their care and also the quality of their program.

One implication of my study is that staff and students who have a strong sense of professional, creative imagination are likely to provide creative, imaginative, and better quality programs for children. How then can we select staff and students who have a positive professional creative imagination?

Creativity, Imagination, and Enchantment Indicators

There are indicators that allow the ranking of potential staff or students in their professional, creative imagination. These are reflected in a person's disposi-

tion and may be discovered through their comments, emotions, and responses in interviews or through the process of creating a personal vision as outlined below. Indicators may also appear in their work, what they do with children, their thinking processes, and their own sense of reflection.

Begin by asking a prospective teacher to create her own personal vision of her ideal children's program:

"Create in your mind a wonderful setting where children are able to learn, have fun, cry, explore, and grow. Imagine in your dream that you are moving among the children and other adults. Live your dream. Use all your perceptive skills to discover what makes your vision so wonderful for children." (Broinowski, 2002, p. 64)

Ask your students or interviewees to explore their ideas using Mind Mapping® techniques. Provide them with plenty of collage materials, paints, glue, natural materials and see what happens.

Allow each person to talk through her ideas and in the process look for her sense of enchantment, imagination, and creativity.

Enchantment

Look for a sense of enchantment in the early childhood educator. To be enchanted is to be delighted or captivated, utterly fascinated, or charmed. This is indicated by an educator's behaviour in such things as:

■ curiosity in ideas, how things work, why things happen, and about the world around them.

■ being engrossed in an event or things happening.

■ keen sense of interest in many diverse areas.

Imagination

Look for indicators of the educator's or professional's imagination. How imaginative are they in their work with young children? How good are they at producing ideas or creating mental images of what is not present or they have not yet experienced? This may be shown in their behaviour by indicators such as:

- divergent thinking.

- inventiveness.

- metaphoric thinking.

- abstract thought.

- holistic senses.

- pretending.

- thinking beyond reality.

Creativity

Look for some evidence that shows the educator's ability to bring new ideas into existence and which directly contribute to the quality of their work with young children. This may be shown by the following indicators (Dalton, 1985, p. 30):

- **Fluency** — thinking of many ideas related to a particular topic.

- **Flexibility** — thinking about a problem by analysing and finding different approaches or ways of seeing the issue.

- **Originality** — including the element of uniqueness.

- **Elaboration** — building onto an idea to make it more interesting or complete.

- **Complexity** — finding many different and challenging alternatives to a problem. It is also the ability to bring some order out of disorganisation and chaos.

- **Risk taking**.

- **Imagination** — allows people to go beyond the boundaries of reality.

The Children's Creative Imagination

The second way to discover a person's sense of creative imagination is simply allow her the freedom and latitude to devise her own program and to observe her at work. An educator's creative imagination is directly reflected in the creative imagination of the children in her play. More precisely, you are trying to determine whether her program creates a learning experience that generates potential for children to extend their creative imagination. Clearly this notion is problematic. Does a lump of playdough on a table by itself have the potential for children to be creative? Children can happily play for hours with just one Lego® person, or with a toy car, or in a pool of mud. It is not the item itself that is creative but rather the creative interaction that the child creates with the object.

There are degrees of potentiality, and, given the right learning environment, children and adults are more likely to be imaginative and creative in their learning. Potentiality for imaginative learning may be seen in child-adult relationships, the environment, and the activity, and may be assessed through observations and discussion.

1. Relationships

Look for the creation of conditions, which inspire children. Things like sharing curiosity; expressing a sense of wonder; valuing children's contributions; incorporating and adapting to children's interest and ideas; helping children focus on their own special talents and strengths.

Think about how they show respect for children. Look for their skills in helping children to explore; offering children secure relationships, which allow curiosity to flourish and seeing the world through the eyes of children (Duffy, 1998, p. 99). Do they value and emphasise the process as well as the product?

2. Environment

The second significant factor providing the basis for imagination and creativity in young children is the environment. Consider the adult's use of spaces and resources. Look at her design for the environment. Is there time and space for the child to work alone or with groups of children and with adults? Is there a variety of materials for exploration and play? What materials spark exploration and play?

How well does the person ensure that there is enough time and space for the child to work alone as well as with groups of children and with adults? Are children given adequate time in which to develop, explore ideas, and be given encouragement?

3. The Activity

The final factor for imaginative and creative learning potential is the activity itself. Cecil et al. (1985, cited in Duffy, 1998, p. 81) presented an interesting way to support the creative process with four elements: curiosity, exploration, play, and creativity.

Curiosity. What is it? Children are alert, interested, and want to know more. Their attention has been captured.

Exploration. What does it do? Children can be observed actively investigating objects, events, or ideas. They are using all their senses to gather information. Watching others can also be part of their investigation.

Play. What can I do with this? Children initiate a period of total immersion characterised by spontaneity and often without clear final objectives.

Creativity. What can children create or invent? The child discovers uncommon or new approaches to the materials or problem they are investigating, they take risks and make new connections.

Conclusion

There is something intrinsically and innately unique about exceptional early childhood educators. Like brilliant artists, they bring something very special to their work. Their presence will add a dimension of rare beauty, wonder, and enchantment in a children's program. By exploring some of the ideas in this article, you may be in a better position to find such a person for your program.

I would love to hear from anyone who would like to try out some of these ideas or simply wants to comment. Write to Ian Broinowski: ianb@our.net.au.

References

Anning, A., & Edward, L. (1999). *Promoting children's learning from birth to five: Developing the new early years professional.* Buchingham: Open University Press.

Buzan, T. (1995). *The mind map book.* London: BBC Books. Mind Map® is a registered trademark of the Buzan organisation, 1990.

Broinowski, I. (2002). *Creative childcare practice: Program design in early childhood.* Upper Saddle River, NJ: Pearson Education.

Dalton, J. (1985). *Adventures in thinking.* Melbourne: Thomas Nelson.

Duffy, B. (1998). "Supporting Creativity and Imagination in the Early Years." In *Supporting Early Learning,* Hurst, V. & Joseph, J. (Eds.) Buchingham: Open University Press.

Fielding, R. (1983). "Creativity Revisited: Strategies for Developing Potential." *Journal of Art Education, 7,* 2:51-60.

NCAC (National Childcare Accreditation Council). (2001). *NCAC source book.* ACT: National Childcare Accreditation Council.

Tegano, D. W., Moran, III, J. D., & Sawyers, J. K. (1991). *Creativity in early childhood classrooms.* First. NEA Early Childhood Series. United States: National Education Association.

Ian Broinowski

Dr. Ian Broinowski, Ph.D, Med, BA(Soc Wk), BEc, Dip Teach, is currently an advanced skills teacher in children's services at the Institute of TAFE Tasmania in Hobart, Australia. Ian has a background in Economics, Social Work, and Education. He has taught a wide range of subjects in aged care, disability services, children's services, community, and youth work. He worked for a period as a house parent in Bristol, England, and Northern Ireland. He has also held positions as a child welfare officer in Tasmania and NSW. Ian's publications include *Child Care Social Policy and Economics* (1994), *Creative Childcare Practice: Program Design in Early Childhood* (2002), and recently *Managing Children's Services* (2004). He has spent the last five years studying for his Ph.D at the University of South Australia in which he examined the relationship between enchantment, imagination, and creativity and the quality of the work of the early childhood educator. Ian was awarded the Jean Denton National Scholarship in 2001.

Interviewing: A Pedagogical Approach

by Anne Marie Coughlin

Author Note: You should always seek the advice of a Human Resources or legal professional if you have questions about the hiring process.

Hiring new educators can be a tiring and difficult process. Often directors are left with short notice, limited choices, and mounting pressures to fill positions. Yet the hiring process is one of the most important things a director can do. The influences of who we hire are far-reaching and extend well past the hiring process itself. The ability for a centre/organization to work towards goals and be successful largely depends on the strength of its people. A poor choice in hiring may provide a warm body in the classroom, but it can also be the cause of many problems in the future.

In our work, it is important for us to parallel what we do with adults with the work we expect adults to do with children in the classrooms. We have built an entire professional development structure around the notion that adult learners deserve the same things as child learners: to be respected, to be seen as being full of potential, to have opportunities to develop theories and work through problems, and to have access to multiple resources. So the question

has occurred to us, "How can we link the interview process to the same theoretical practices we use in the classroom? How might we use the same pedagogical approach to getting to know adults as we do in getting to know children — and do it in a fraction of the time?"

We understand that every child is unique and although we may use a similar approach in getting to know children, it will look different each time. Deb Curtis and Margie Carter often refer to "meeting up with children's minds rather than their behavior." This is valuable insight that has proven incredibly helpful in seeing past what children do to why they are doing it. When we have a greater understanding of what children really mean, it leaves doors open to assist them in accessing what they need. The irony is that by determining and addressing what children are thinking rather than how they are behaving, we are much better positioned to help them make positive behavioural changes that are authentic and helpful to them, and ultimately lead to the building of stronger relationships. And it occurs to us that these same principles apply when working with adults and it begins before a teacher is even hired.

Pedagogical Interviewing

In our classrooms, the adults plan out big ideas and then watch closely how children engage. We observe, document, and interpret both the children's responses to what we offer and what each child's ideas are. Curriculum is ultimately built through a continuous dance between what the child is interested in and what the goals of the teacher are.

The same approach can be effective during the interview process. While the big ideas (or goals) of the interviewer are the same, each candidate is unique and will enter the process differently, each having their own interests, challenges, and strengths. Our job in the interview process is to observe, document, and interpret in the same way teachers would in the classroom. The challenge, of course, is in constructing an interview that can help determine the right person for the job considering the relatively short time period that many of us are afforded for interviewing and hiring.

Identify Your Big Ideas

Best practice in the classroom acknowledges that while teachers have big ideas and goals, their work with each child is an emergent process that is responsive to the individuality of each child. In our view, the same is true of the interview process. It is important to identify your own big ideas regarding what you want in an employee. These ideas should consider not simply what you are looking for in the immediate future, but the long term as well:

- What dispositions are important for you?

- What are the things that you can help develop in an employee?

- What are the things that you require from the get go?

Once you have identified what you are looking for, try formulating questions around those ideas. Some of the big ideas we have focused on in our work include:

- knowledge of child development.

- ability to form strong relationships.

- capacity to collaborate and work with others.

- commitment to lifelong learning.

- strong image of the child.

Under each idea we might develop two or three questions that would be asked of every candidate. Then, depending on the experiences of the individual, more individualized questions will emerge. Just as in the classroom, these questions cannot be predicted ahead of time as they arise in response to a unique answer from a candidate.

Using the Principles of Observation, Documentation, and Interpretation

In the classroom we strive to listen, observe, and take notes and photographs all in an attempt to collect data that we can later interpret and make meaning of. The value in this process is that we give ourselves time to think and avoid jumping to immediate judgment.

It occurs to me that the same principles should be true of the interview process. We ask questions, we listen, we take notes, and we interpret. However, what often happens is we jump to judgment quickly. Instead of giving ourselves time to collect data, we all too often make assumptions about the competencies and appropriateness of the candidate. If we are not careful, it can be too easy to both rule out an appropriate person or hire an inappropriate one. Listed are some tips:

■ Ask questions and listen and document answers.

■ Allow candidates' responses to emerge into new questions.

■ As you begin to interpret and develop theories, develop new questions to test your theories.

■ Avoid making judgments during the interview; judgments turn to bias and then you begin to see exactly what you are looking for. Instead, make interpretations and test them out.

For example: If a candidate is shy and nervous, I might make a judgment that she would have trouble forming relationships. In this case, I will find all kinds of evidence in her responses that confirm my perception of her.

Likewise, if she is eager and talkative, I might make an instant judgment that she will be a great team player. My follow-up questions will set out to confirm this.

■ Ideally, it is best to interview with someone else with whom you can compare perspectives and make meaning together.

Interpreting behaviours and answers is distinctly different from judging them; one is open and leads to testing theories to see if they are accurate, while the other is closed and simply seeks out more evidence that supports the judgment.

Learning What They Know: Using Behaviour-based Questioning

In our work with children, it is always important to begin by learning what they already know. The whole point of an interview is based on the same idea — to learn what a candidate knows.

Considering the short amount of time that an interview offers, a great way to explore what a candidate knows is by asking behaviour-based questions. Behaviour-based questions require a person to draw

on what they have already done rather than what they might do. These types of questions are far more valuable in understanding how a person thinks, what motivates them, and what their values are. Anyone can provide textbook answers or offer explanations of what they think you want to hear; but when they tell the story of their own experience, it offers opportunities to emerge into a richer conversation that will help paint a fuller portrait of who this person is. This can be done simply by changing a question from, "What would you do if…" to "Tell me about a time when you…."

In my experience, these questions can be difficult for people to respond to. Interviewees are often not used to this type of questioning and will often answer behaviour-based questions with, "I would…" statements. I always find it effective to explain right from the beginning of the interview what I am looking for; if they give "I would" answers, I remind them that we want them to draw on actual experiences.

Be Aware of the Pitfalls

Striving for a quick fix: Hiring too quickly. Often there can be tremendous pressure from both teachers and parents to hire someone quickly. However, it is important to remember that moving too fast can result in hiring the wrong person for the job. This can lead to even more difficulties in the future.

Remind teachers and parents that this is an incredibly important decision and that they and the children deserve to have the best possible person in place. Time and energy spent in the beginning is the best way to build a strong team.

Hiring for a coworker. I have often heard directors describe the person they are looking for as 'fitting' with the coworker they will be potentially working with. While I understand the importance of building relationships among coworkers, I have come to understand that often we are trying to compensate for another individual's weakness by placing them with someone who can either offset or tolerate it. In many cases this can be very appropriate, especially when it comes to consciously supporting each other's learning. However, we need to be very careful not to discount hiring one person because of the challenges of another. If we do, we can run the risk of both missing out on hiring a great teacher and failing to build the competences and accountability of a current staff member.

Gut instinct and personal bias. While going by gut instinct can sometimes serve us, often it is short-sighted and filled with bias. I once sat in on an interview with a director who was looking for a long-term employee who had a strong knowledge of child development. Instead, she was swept off her feet by a young teacher with no experience and who was extraordinarily sweet and well-dressed; but it was very clear that she had no intention of staying on past a year. Identifying our own bias and the assumptions that accompany them can be very helpful in avoiding unfair judgments of prospective employees. Consider your thoughts about age, weight, culture and ethnicity, gender, and physical appearance of staff. Identify your blind spots and biases in order to give all candidates equal opportunity to present their qualifications for your review.

It is often said that the majority of the work is done in the planning stage, and this rings true for the hiring process. It may be only a first step, but it is by far the most significant in building a long and rewarding working relationship.

Anne Marie Coughlin

Over her 25-year career Anne Marie Coughlin has worked as a classroom educator, a centre director, professional development coordinator, and college faculty. For the past 10 years she has been a Director of Program Leadership at London Bridge Child Care Services, one of the largest child care organizations in Ontario, Canada, and has been instrumental in developing several innovative professional development initiatives including an 18-month leadership development program. Anne Marie continues to mentor classroom educators and program leaders, exploring ways to work with and think about both children's and adults' learning.

Summary

As leaders, our job is to help other educators be successful in their work. It is imperative that we see them as competent capable learners, that we help them feel a sense of belonging, and hold them accountable to the values of the centre, just as they do with children in the classroom.

Just as teachers' work is critical with children, our work is critical with teachers. This work begins before an employee is even hired. As a leader, you are a living role model and mentor to your staff from the first moment you meet.

Questions that Get You Great Teachers

by Jennifer Carsen

High-quality teachers who are a good fit with your program and who stay with you for the long haul can seem as elusive as the Loch Ness Monster. These teachers are worth their weight in gold in terms of the experience and continuity they bring to your program, as well as the peace of mind they bring to parents.

Unless you are very, very lucky, these teachers won't just show up at your doorstep by chance. You need to hire them — and the right hires start with the right interview questions.

The Pre-interview

So you've posted your job opening, you've sorted through the applications, and you've identified a few candidates you're pretty excited about. The next step is to ask these people to come in for an interview, right? Wrong. Many applicants look good on paper, but don't hold up nearly as well in person. To save everyone's time — yours as well as the applicants' — make interviewing a two-step process, with the first interview scheduled as a 15-minute phone call.

Have the applicant call you rather than the other way around. That way, you can automatically eliminate anyone who calls in late (or not at all)! This may sound harsh, but anyone who isn't prompt and proactive about an initial phone interview — a time when she should be eager to impress — is not likely to be a superstar employee.

What should you ask during this pre-interview? This is a good time to gather more general information about the applicant, clarify any questions you may have about her application or credentials, and get an overall sense of whether a second, in-person interview is warranted. At this stage, you want to be evaluating the applicant's poise and professionalism, too: Does this sound like a person you'd be comfortable having speak to current and prospective parents?

Good questions for the telephone pre-interview:

- **What first attracted you to this position?** Watch out for answers that are all about why the position is good for the applicant rather than what she can do for you.

- **Why are you leaving your current/previous position?** Beware applicants who badmouth former employers or supervisors.

- **Can you tell me about this gap in your résumé?** It's best to address potential red flags like this earlier, rather than later.

■ **Do you have any questions for me about the position?** Again, watch out for self-serving questions ("How much time off will I get?"). Ideally, the applicant will have at least a few questions for you, and those questions will reveal that she has done some homework. For example, strong applicants will ask questions relating to something they saw on your website, rather than asking, "Do you have a website?"

The Main Event

Good news! Your applicant has cleared the telephone interview with flying colors, and you're excited to meet in person.

Child care centers can be hectic places, but in order to get the most out of the interview experience you must be prepared to focus on it 100%. Plan to have someone else answer the phone during your interviews, and be clear that you are not to be interrupted, except for an emergency. You need to be able to focus your full attention on the candidate, and she, in turn, deserves a chance to shine. Additionally, even candidates who are accustomed to the hectic atmosphere of a busy child care center will be turned off by a constant stream of interruptions during a job interview; it makes you appear unprofessional.

If there's no way to guarantee an interruption-free interview at your center, hold it off-site — maybe at a nearby coffee shop. Then, if there is still mutual interest at the conclusion of the interview, bring the candidate over to your center for a tour. Note that the tour itself is a good opportunity to observe how the applicant interacts with both her prospective co-workers and the children at your center. Being comfortable with young children, and excited about spending time with them, is a skill that's very difficult to fake.

In addition, promising applicants are polite and respectful to everyone they encounter during the interview — whether it's a parent, a teacher, a child, or even the vendor servicing your balky boiler. Curt or dismissive behavior directed towards someone the applicant perceives as unimportant (due to the person's lack of involvement in the hiring process) provides a revealing glimpse into her character.

Finally, if at all possible, have another administrator or master teacher present for the interviews. She will be able to ask questions you may not have thought of, and will also be able to provide an additional perspective after the interviews are over.

Depending on your management style and the formality level of your center, you may wish to conduct the interview seated in adjacent chairs, or across a low table, rather than on opposite sides of your desk. This can make the interview more relaxed and conversational, and applicants tend to open up more in this type of setting.

Interview Questions: The Good

Ultimately, the best interview questions help reveal both who the applicant really is, and how she would perform on the job. Always ask open-ended questions, rather than those with "yes" or "no" answers, and avoid leading questions where the correct answer is implied. For example, "How do you enjoy working in a close-knit team environment?" No candidate is going to respond, "I don't!" to that one.

Some good questions:

■ **Scenario-based:** "You've just heard one of the preschoolers tell a classmate that his dark skin is 'dirty.' How do you respond?" or "You strongly suspect a child in your class may have autism and recommend an assessment to his parents, but they say he's fine and that they don't want to take the time away from work. What do you do?"

■ **What accomplishments are you most proud of in your life?** Everyone has something they can — and should — be proud of, and the best candidates will probably be able to talk about more than one thing.

■ **Where do you see yourself in five years?** There's no single right answer to this question, but the answer is always illuminating. "I have no idea" is never a good answer. Neither is something like, "I see myself as a manager at a large corporation" if you're looking for a long-term hire.

■ **What would your previous (or current) manager say your strengths and weaknesses are?** This one is illuminating as it requires an additional level of thinking beyond the candidate's own self-assessment.

■ **What did you like most and least about your previous job?** The answer will reveal not only the applicant's job and task preferences, but also her professionalism and level of diplomacy.

■ **How do you resolve personal conflicts at work?** Every job presents challenges in working with others. Strong applicants recognize this and will have developed strategies for effectively addressing — rather than avoiding — them.

Interview Questions: The Bad

The following sorts of questions don't tend to elicit a lot of helpful information:

■ **If you were a tree, what kind of tree would you be?** Whatever the applicant answers, it's probably not going to tell you anything useful.

■ **What's your favorite animal, and why?** If you're hoping for the applicant to reveal something about a desired characteristic ("I like mules because they're very tenacious!"), it's much better to ask about that characteristic directly. For example, "Tell me about a time in your previous work history when tenacity paid off for you.")

■ **What are your weaknesses?** Applicants have been conditioned to spin a negative into a positive here ("I'm a relentless perfectionist!"), so you're not going to get a truthful answer. No job applicant is going to volunteer info about his spending problem, or her procrastination.

■ **How do you feel about workplace gossip?** Again, even if she is an enthusiastic participant in workplace gossip, the applicant is not going to level with you on this one. Additionally, this type of question can make applicants worry that your workplace has a gossip problem — which will drive away the strongest candidates.

■ **Tell me about yourself.** This is too broad, and too vague to elicit the type of information you're seeking in an interview situation. Also, it opens the door wide for disclosures about the applicant that you're better off not knowing from a legal standpoint (more on this in the next section).

Interview Questions: The Ugly

Sometimes, especially in a people-oriented field like child care, interview chit-chat can wander into illegal territory. You should always avoid questions relating — even tangentially — to an applicant's marital status, religion, age, ethnicity, disability, or other protected characteristic:

■ Are you married?

■ Do you have kids?

■ Do you attend church regularly?

■ Are you planning to start a family soon?

■ Is your spouse supportive of the long commute you'll have if you work here?

■ How old are you?

■ When did you graduate from high school/college?

■ Do you live with anyone?

■ You have an interesting accent/last name. Where is your family from?

If you have a legitimate job-related concern, ask about it directly. For example, "We'd need you to rearrange the classroom furniture from time to time, and some of the tables weigh 25 pounds. Would you be able to do that?" is legally safe. "Do you have any physical disabilities?" is not.

Final Tips

It's important to ask all candidates the same questions, both so you are comparing apples with apples when reviewing your notes, and also to avoid any potential allegations of illegal bias down the line.

Keep detailed notes, but make sure that all of your notes are job-related. You never want to write down something like 'middle-aged Latina woman' or 'gay man,' even if it's just to help jog your memory about which candidate is which.

Ask all candidates for references, and be sure to actually check those references. While many former employers will play it safe and only confirm the dates of past employment — which itself can be valuable information — some will volunteer more. Always ask, "Would this candidate be eligible for re-hire with you?"

Finally, regardless of how great someone seems during the interview, resist the urge to offer the person the position right then and there. Sleep on it before making a final decision.

Jennifer Carsen

Jennifer Carsen is the founder of Daycare In Demand, which specializes in working with preschools and child care centers to grow their enrollments and attract/retain the very best teachers. She is a member of the National Association for the Education of Young Children and the American Society of Journalists and Authors. Jennifer is a former employment lawyer who was named a "Top 25 Online Influencer in Employment Law" by HR Examiner in 2012. She is a member of the New Hampshire Bar Association and the author of *HR How-to: Employee Retention* (CCH, 2005). Visit her website: www.daycareindemand.com.

Observing Teaching Candidates in Action

by Roger Neugebauer

"We found that everyone loves children in the abstract, but will they love them eight hours a day in the classroom?" Thus Nancy Alexander explained the reason her center in Shreveport, Louisiana, instituted a policy of observing all teaching candidates before they were hired. At first, when teachers were selected strictly on the basis of their interviews, she found that there often was a wide variance between how individuals described their child caring skills and how they actually performed in action. By observing likely candidates working in a center, Nancy Alexander was able to much more reliably assess them. As a result, she nearly eliminated hiring mistakes.

This experience is not unique. Most early childhood programs now include observations as an integral part of their selection procedures. To provide readers with ideas on how to conduct an effective observation, *Exchange* surveyed eight child care organizations that have experienced positive results with this staff selection technique. The results of this survey are summarized below.

Before the Observation

An observation can provide a reasonably reliable forecast of a candidate's likely performance if it is properly prepared for. This preparation should center around the identification of what you hope to learn about candidates in the observations.

You probably can generate a long list of qualifications you would like to find in your ideal teaching candidate. Some of these, such as **level of training**, can be reliably measured by a résumé review; and others, such as **knowledge of child development**, can be assessed well in interviews. Many others, especially those relating to personality traits and teaching style, can only be assessed by observing the candidates in action. Identify a few of these qualifications or traits that are most critical to the accomplishment of your center's curriculum goals. Don't attempt to assess too many or your attention will be dispersed in too many directions to effectively measure anything.

For each trait, identify some specific indicators to look for during the observation. For example, if an important qualification is **positive interaction skills**, helpful indicators of this might be **maintains eye**

contact at the child's level and listens patiently to children. At the end of this article are listed 29 such indicators that the surveyed directors found to yield insightful data on the candidates.

Thoroughly discuss the list of qualifications and their indicators in a staff meeting. Make sure that anyone who will participate in observations understands what to look for. Make any revisions that come out of this discussion for improving or clarifying the list. Then print it up in a checklist format to hand to observers before each observation to be sure the traits and indicators are attended to.

With this degree of preparation, observation can be a more reliable staff selection technique than the interview. It would be desirable to be able to observe all candidates who meet the center's minimum training and experience standards. This might enable you to identify candidates who don't have impressive formal qualifications and who do not express themselves skillfully in the interview but who, nevertheless, are naturally gifted in interacting with children. Unfortunately, observations are time consuming and a bit disruptive to the flow of classroom activities. Therefore, most centers tend to use observations sparingly — only observing the top two to five candidates from the interviews. If this is the approach your center must take, follow your hunches from time to time. Include among those to be observed candidates who didn't fare well through the interview stage, but who you have a gut feeling may do well in practice.

Bea Ganson, a director in Abilene, Texas, is able to get a maximum use of observations by requiring all candidates to serve as paid substitutes before they can be hired. Thus she can observe many candidates over a period of time before making selection decisions.

During the Observation

One teaching candidate, upon inquiring at a center about a job, was immediately assigned for his *observation* to care for 15 children in the nap room by himself. Many of the children could not be comforted by this *stranger*, and most of the others took the opportunity to test him. The result was chaos. The candidate had a miserable experience and never considered returning to that center, and the center didn't get the foggiest picture of what the candidate was like as a teacher.

For the best results, the center should schedule observations carefully. Centers have found that observations should last at least two to four hours to get a reliable picture of a candidate. Shorter periods do not allow candidates enough time to get acclimated.

Time of day is also critical. Nancy Alexander schedules interviews during a free play period rather than a group activity time so that candidates are more likely to get involved with the children instead of sitting back and observing an activity. Peg Persinger, a director in Eugene, Oregon, tends to assign candidates to the most challenging groups to really test their skills. Most directors also assign candidates to work with teachers they would actually be working with if they were hired, so current teachers can assess whether this is someone they would be comfortable with.

In any event, try to have all candidates for a single position be observed by the same staff people. Barbara Day, a director in Edmonton, Alberta, recommends scheduling all observations for a single position in the same week so that the memories of the first candidates won't fade by the time the last ones are observed.

For the candidate to present a true picture of herself, she needs to be as relaxed and comfortable as possible. For the candidate to be interested in working for the center, she needs to have as pleasant an experience as possible. Both these requirements call for the director to take specific steps to put the candidate at ease about the observation and to ease her into it gently. Start by telling all candidates from the beginning that they may be expected to participate in an observation. When scheduling interviews, tell them exactly what will be expected of them, how long the observation will last, and what the class is like that they will be in.

On the day of the observation, the director should escort the candidate into the room and introduce her to the teaching staff and the children. At this point, Barbara Day leaves the candidate, and the supervisor (or head teacher) leads the candidate on a brief tour of the room.

The candidate's involvement in the activity of the room should be allowed to expand gradually. Most centers allow for a 30-minute *warm-up period* in which no official observations are made. Candidates under observation at the North Pocono Preschool in North Pocono, Pennsylvania, are encouraged by director Gail Laskowski to start their four-hour observation by observing what is going on for a while, then working with the teachers for a while, and finally working on their own when they feel comfortable doing so.

Many centers ask the candidates to plan and present a specific 20- to 40-minute activity for the children. Karen Miller, Evergreen, Colorado, has found that if some of the less experienced candidates are not given such a specific task, they tend to sit around, giving no hint of their potential. Staff should go out of their way to cooperate with the candidates in providing materials and assistance for the activities. Give the candidates every opportunity to do their best.

During the observation, it is best not to heighten their sense of being followed by all eyes. The director should not pull up a chair and formally observe the whole period. Gail Laskowski simply makes a point of being in the area with a purpose, often during this period. The teachers should also go on about their business and not take notes or talk about the candidate in her presence.

On the other hand, the staff should not ignore the candidate, but should be alert to her performance. While observers should take note of a candidate's general demeanor, they should most keenly observe

how he handles specific incidents. The data they should be trying to collect is not general impressions, but as many small pieces of evidence as possible — especially pieces of evidence relating to the indicators identified beforehand.

After the Observation

There should be a definite closure to the observation. The director should return to the room to retrieve the candidate, or the head teacher should thank her and ask her to report back to the director. At this point, Barbara Day invites the candidate to share her reactions. These reactions can be very revealing. The candidate's impressions of specific incidents can disclose a great deal about her knowledge and philosophy. For example, the candidate may talk about the *misbehavior* of a certain *troublemaker* when in reality this child's behavior was well within normal bounds. This may be a clue to you that either this candidate is not tuned in to child development or else she may have a more restrictive approach than you prefer. If the candidate shares only general reactions, it may be useful to prod her memory with open-ended statements about specific incidents.

After the candidate leaves, all those who observed her should take the first opportunity to record their reactions. Gail Laskowski has all observers rate the candidate on a selection criteria matrix and then include some narrative comments.

Then, as soon as possible, while the experience is still fresh in everyone's minds, the observers should meet together to share their assessments. The director should steer this discussion away from generalities. One way to do this is to read through the list of traits and their indicators. For each indicator, ask observers to describe specific incidents where this indicator was demonstrated in a negative or positive way. If the indicator relates to the candidate's success in integrating children into the group, the observers would describe a candidate's various attempts to do so and the outcome of the attempts. By reviewing as much specific evidence as possible, the observers will eventually have a reasonably solid basis for deciding whether or not to hire the candidate.

Observations can add a strong element of reliability to staff selection decisions. However, this technique does not guarantee that all mistakes will be avoided. Charlene Richardson, director of the Child Development Center in San Diego, places new employees on a three-month probationary status. During this period, she carefully monitors their performance using the same procedures as in the selection observation. Such pre- and post-hiring observations do require considerable effort on the part of staff members; but in the long run, they assure a more consistent program for the children.

What to Look For

The directors surveyed for this article identified the following performance indicators as ones they have used with the best results. Overall, the indicators that were cited most frequently related to the way the candidates relate to the children. As Nancy Alexander explained, "We want to see if they treat them as sweet cutesies or as thinking human beings." In this vein, the most popular indicators were tone of voice, eye contact, body language, and listening skills.

Physical Appearance and Personal Attitude:

■ Does she use positive body language?

■ Is her tone of voice appropriate?

■ What are her facial expressions as she interacts with children? Is she animated, angry, or "bored to tears"?

■ Does she maintain eye contact at the child's level?

■ Does she dress appropriately, "as if she expects to sit on the floor and have tempera paint spilled over her?"

■ Does she convey an overall sense of enthusiasm?

■ Is she having fun or is she tense and resentful?

Interaction Skills:

■ How does she react when children approach her?

■ How does she answer children's questions?

■ Does she listen carefully and patiently to what children tell her? How does she signal interest in their communications?

■ Does she appear comfortable talking to children?

■ Does she serve as a good language model?

■ How does she help integrate children into the group?

Direction and Control:

■ Does she maintain control? How?

■ How does she show tolerance for child-like demands, impatience, mood swings, self-assertion, negativism, exuberance, angry feelings, tears, and testing behavior? How does she guide children at such times toward adequate coping and socially acceptable behavior?

■ Does she allow children to resolve their own conflicts?

■ How much are children allowed to diverge from her directions?

■ If a child has lost control, can the candidate accept the child's feelings and help him regain control? Does she retaliate or offer alternatives? Does she tear the child down or build him up?

■ Does the candidate use a positive approach — "Blocks are for building" — or are her directives negative — "Don't throw that block."

Teaching Skills:

■ Is she actively engaged or merely babysitting?

■ If she brings in an activity, is it appropriate for the age group she is working with?

■ Is she able to follow a schedule while still remaining flexible?

■ Is she able to adjust to unforeseen incidents?

■ How well does she hold the interest of the children?

■ How well does she arouse children's curiosity?

■ Does she move around the room to help children and show interest in what they are doing?

■ Does she provide an appropriate balance of unstructured and structured activities?

■ Does she demonstrate a willingness to learn, herself? Is she open to new ideas? Does she ask questions about particular activities and materials?

■ Does she work comfortably with other staff in the room?

Roger Neugebauer

Roger Neugebauer is publisher of *Exchange Magazine* and a co-founder of the World Forum Foundation.

Hiring and Retaining Male Staff

by Bruce Cunningham

> "We advertise for teachers all the time, but no men ever apply."
>
> "We have one male teacher, but I'm afraid he'll leave our program."

Directors who make these comments acknowledge the challenges in hiring and retaining male staff. While there are relatively small numbers of well-qualified men who can teach young children, there are also effective ways of recruiting them.

Hiring men requires a change in recruitment strategies, and retaining men requires a change in workplace practices. Yet an intentional approach to recruiting and supporting male staff can be successful — and the results can make your program more diverse and responsive to the needs of young children.

Advertising for Men

Due to the cost of classified advertisements, most programs keep the wording to a minimum, speaking only to the most important or required qualifications of education and experience. When additional descriptive words are used, it is to acknowledge something about the nature of the work — such as using the word *energetic*, which speaks to the physically demanding nature of the work in the most cheery way possible.

Occasionally, other descriptors are used, and these most commonly include *nurturing, caring, affectionate*, and *gentle*. These are important characteristics, and most programs have staff that exemplifies them. However, if you are interested in attracting men and diversifying the characteristics of your staff, consider using words that are more attractive to men. These words include *physically active, outdoors, fun*, and *socially important work*. Many men think in terms of this last phrase to rationalize the low wages they receive.

Advertising directly for male staff with the words *Men Wanted* is unacceptable to most newspapers. Yet it is an acceptable practice to add a line to the advertisement that says "Men encouraged to apply." The reason for this is that the standard for child care positions is women and this line draws the attention of the advertisement to a target audience of men without excluding women.

Such a line is similar to other frequently seen phrases such as *Equal opportunity employer, Committed to workplace diversity,* and, particularly in higher education, *Women and minorities encouraged to apply.* However, in this case, the intent is not one of affirmative action — to provide employment opportunity to members of a group who have previously been excluded. Instead, the intent is to provide children with the presence of men. The additional cost of this phrase will likely be the cost of adding one more line to the classified advertisement — the price of which will vary from newspaper to newspaper.

Most classified advertisements are placed under the categories of day care, child care, preschool, teachers, or education. These are appropriate places for the position, but are not the first places many men tend to look. An alternative strategy is to place advertisements in categories that men will be more likely to see. These categories include activities coordinator, recreational supervisor, playground supervisor, computer applications with children, or general labor. The idea is that an entry-level position of teacher aide or teacher assistant in many programs has important, but very general, qualifications.

Advertising the position in a way that will bring it to the attention of men is a first step in getting men to apply for the position. This idea need not be deceptive when the advertisement also includes more detailed information that is also given to potential applicants making phone inquiries and to those actually applying.

Another strategy for placing advertisements is to seek out alternative publications in the community. Many larger cities, for example, have a men's organization that distributes a newsletter with articles about men's issues, events, gatherings, support groups, and other services of interest to men. While the circulation of these publications will be small and not approach the circulation of a daily newspaper, the readership will be almost entirely male.

Asking the Right Questions

In a job interview, it is important to ask questions that elicit information about the qualifications of the applicant. Yet, when a man is interviewed, particularly by a panel of women, he may be reluctant to admit a lack of experience or he may not recognize relevant experiences that apply to the position. The women who are interviewing the man may subconsciously believe that a man is not entirely capable of working with young children and may not ask enough probing questions.

In this situation, general questions such as "Tell me about yourself" will not reveal the most important kinds of information. More specific questions that lead applicants to speak about relevant experiences are needed, and these include:

Have you worked around young children or youth before? Have you been involved . . .

■ *in sports as a coach or referee?*

■ *in swimming lessons or as a lifeguard?*

■ *as a playground supervisor or recreational supervisor?*

■ *in a church youth group?*

■ *as a counselor at a summer camp or an outdoor school?*

■ *with a scouting group?*

■ *in babysitting younger siblings or neighborhood children?*

When the man answers yes to one of these questions, it is important to follow up with more probing questions to find out how the involvement in these activities applies to the position. Such questions include:

What kinds of things did you do? Did you . . .

■ *plan activities?*

■ *teach a skill?*

- *supervise children? how many? what ages? for how long at a time?*

- *enforce rules? discipline children? break up a fight?*

- *keep written records? attendance? scores? an activity log?*

- *care for equipment? what kind of equipment?*

- *meet parents? explain activities to parents?*

Retaining Men

Once men are hired, it is important to retain them. Many men who are the only man on a staff of women experience feelings of isolation (Nelson & Sheppard, 1992). Yet men will stay in an environment they feel is equitable, safe, values men, and supports them in personal and professional growth.

If you have a man on staff, make sure the assignment of tasks to men and women is equitable. For example, is male staff able to work with all age groups of children rather than just the older groups of children? Does male staff have the opportunity to work with different groups of children or is the man placed with the children most in need of guidance in the assumption that he will provide the guidance that is needed? Are men automatically scheduled to spend more time on the playground than female staff? Men may enjoy spending more time out of doors, but often resent being automatically expected to do so.

Think about other job-related tasks such as taking out the garbage, lifting heavy objects, and changing light bulbs in high places. Of course men will do these things, but will certainly resent always being expected to do so.

Consider whether men are allowed the same freedom in their individual teaching style as are women. Many male teachers develop a style that includes activities that are more physically active, louder, messier, and involve more humor, joking, and

silliness. This style is appropriate under the broad umbrella of developmentally appropriate practices and can be a valuable addition to the styles of other teachers in a program.

Men will continue to work in an environment in which they feel safe and protected. Many men feel they are but one false accusation away from having to leave a satisfying career working with young children. It is important to have policies that protect men — and all staff — such as those specifying that no staff person is left alone with a child.

Men also feel protected when they receive support from their supervisors. This is particularly important when parents raise questions about the appropriateness of a man doing certain tasks such as diapering infants and toddlers. A supervisor can use such an opportunity to educate the parents by referring to the policy that speaks to the importance of men as competent caregivers. This kind of support affirms the status of a man as a valued member of the staff who can and will perform all tasks required by the profession.

Valuing Men

Male staff is inclined to stay in a work environment that values men. Images of men — such as fathers with children — on posters, bulletin boards, and other wall decorations reflect this importance. Magazines in a staff lounge, a parent lounge, and a lobby area should reflect the interests of men as well as women. Work uniforms can be modified or adapted to emphasize that men are staff members, too. Social activities among staff can include talk and activities that are also of interest to men. A good way to examine the workplace environment is to spend some time answering the question: "What would our program look like if half the staff were men?"

Another way of examining the overall environment is to consider the degree to which it is father friendly (McBride & Rane, 1996). A key idea here is the amount of father involvement your program has generated. For example, *Do as many fathers come to parent activities as mothers?* The attitudes and practices that support the involvement of fathers are the same kinds of things that will retain male staff (Levine, Murphy, & Wilson, 1993).

It is also important that men see the topic of men intentionally included in staff training activities. For example, when diversity is addressed — in any of its many forms of parent involvement, staff working relationships, and multicultural/anti-bias curriculum — make sure the topic of men is included in the discussion. Address and challenge the common assumptions that all evils in our society are the fault of men. Explore the significant contributions men make to child development; debunk the many stereotypes of men as being uncaring or inherently untalented to care for young children.

Examine how our society does not always favor men in that the vast majority of the homeless, alcoholics, substance abusers, and victims of violent crime are men — and that men have a shorter life expectancy than women. In sexual harassment training sessions, make sure that the discussion and the examples given do not always assume that the harasser is a man and the victim is a woman.

Men will want to stay in an environment where they have opportunities for personal and professional growth. Men who are just beginning in the field will appreciate flexibility in their work schedule and tuition support to continue their education. Men who have been in the field for some time will appreciate opportunities, encouragement, and freedom to undertake interesting projects, such as working with different age groups of children to develop new teaching skills, planning innovative curriculum activities or materials, becoming more involved with parent-involvement activities — perhaps in the form of a father-and-child event or ongoing series of father-and-child activity nights.

Male staff also feels less isolated when they have the opportunity to interact with other men in the field. The presence of more than one man on a staff and the presence of fathers and male volunteers have a snowball effect, which makes the environment increasingly friendly towards men. Consider sponsoring a group of male teachers who wish to meet on a regular basis by providing space for a meeting, or supporting the publicity of such a group through a mailing, or providing a continental breakfast or refreshments for such a meeting.

Getting the Word Out

A variety of other strategies can be used to attract men. These include:

- Encourage your staff to recruit applicants for vacant positions. This word-of-mouth advertising can be effective when linked to cash incentives. Typically such incentives include a cash reward to the employee at the time the person he or she referred signs a contract. Another reward (sometimes split between the two employees) may be made when the new employee, in this case a man, completes a probationary period.

- Establish a résumé bank of potential male applicants. Invite currently employed men and men in teacher-training programs to submit résumés and then inform them as positions become vacant.

Finally, it is important to support worthy wage and cost, quality, and affordability initiatives. One of the reasons many men give for not entering or for leaving this field is the low wages. Men, and all staff, need to know that this is an issue that is being addressed.

References

Levine, J., Murphy, D., & Wilson, S. (1993). *Getting men involved: Strategies for early childhood programs.* New York: Scholastic Inc.

McBride, B., & Rane, T. (1996). "Father/Male involvement in early childhood programs." ERIC/EECE Digest, EDO-PS-96-10.

Nelson, B., & Sheppard, B. (1992). *Men in child care and early education.* Stillwater, MN: nu ink press.

Acknowledgments

Several individuals contributed to this article by previewing earlier drafts and offering additional ideas and feedback. They are: Bryan Nelson, Wendy Roedell, Bruce Sheppard, Gregory Uba, and Steve Weber.

Bruce Cunningham

Bruce Cunningham has worked in early childhood settings as an assistant, a teacher, a director, and an educator. He is currently an education coordinator with the Early Childhood Education and Assistance Program (ECEAP) through the Puget Sound Educational Service District in Seattle, Washington.

Bringing Diversity into Your Center

by Thomas Moore

> No matter where your child care center is located, chances are it fits the following description:
> If you're white, virtually everyone else in your center is white, too.
> If you're African-American, you have mostly an African-American clientele and staff.

You're not alone. Most child care centers in the United States have teachers and administrators who look the same and come from similar backgrounds. Anyone who has tried it knows it's a challenge to develop a multiracial staff and attract children from all racial and religious groups.

But I believe it can be done. And it's worth the effort. With many kinds of people involved, a child care center becomes appealing to a wider range of people, leading to new marketing opportunities and greater financial stability. A diverse staff is more likely to help families of every hue feel welcome in your facility and, ultimately, chooses to pay for your services. Families who are uncomfortable with diversity might latch onto a staff member with a similar background. The person who connects with those parents can ease their way into a new and ultimately rewarding setting.

Children learn more and have more fun with the opportunity to explore different cultures. Teachers and administrators do, too. Our differences can be jumping-off points for learning, growth, and development for all of us. It's harder to discuss the mountains when everyone in the group grew up at the beach. It's harder to convey the taste of tortillas if everyone was born in Maine.

A diverse child care center is the ultimate expression of the motto "Think globally, act locally." It is a vital first step to bringing people together to talk about who we are and what we can create together. It's one means for creating "a world that holds their children dear and loves them as they are" (from "A Dream for Children," a song by Drs. Jan McCarthy and Thomas Moore).

Getting Started

Even after a center has made the choice to seek a diverse staff and clientele, it still can be difficult to *practice what you preach.*

Consider the experiences of Anne Jones, director of the Avondale Children's Center in Charlotte, North Carolina. When Jones joined Avondale three years ago, she came from a center that had been diverse for several decades, thanks to its location, scholarship monies, and other factors. At Avondale, though three out of 11 teachers are African-American and the center has made diversity a priority; all but one of the children served are white. "It's a puzzle that bothers me, the board, and the church we're affiliated with," Jones says. "We've looked at it inside and out. We're just not getting a diverse group of applicants."

Broadening Your Appeal

Whether you haven't consciously sought out a diverse population before, or you've been frustrated by limited success or outright failure, these strategies can help broaden your center's appeal.

What do they see? Remember that at all times we are either inviting people to join us or we are turning them away. Do prospects see a variety of faces in the pictures on your walls? What about the illustrations in books? Images can be a powerful way to communicate "We want you here."

Diversity goes beyond race. A friend tells the story of her search for child care. She and her husband were touring a well-regarded secular child care center affiliated with a community college. She was impressed until she came to the classroom where children were gathered in a circle, listening to a recording.

"On Sunday, we all go to church, go to church, go to church. On Sunday, we all go the church, early in the morning," sang the voice on the recording. My friend is Jewish. The center's director seemed utterly oblivious to how that recording would be perceived by non-Christians. My friend didn't say anything — and she never went back.

Think diverse personalities. Hire some teachers who are low key, some who are upbeat, some very organized, some very creative. They bring different styles and perspectives to your classrooms, meetings, and interactions with parents. They also serve as diverse role models for children. Kids who are very active, for instance, will benefit by seeing a quieter teacher.

Cultivate hidden diversity. Even if you have families who look alike, there can be diversity in ethnicity, faith, economic class, and interests. Consider asking parents to do short projects or games with children at the center to share the special things they know or do.

An example: one major industry in my community is banking, so children are accustomed to parents who work in an office. To show children that 'the office' isn't the only place people work, one center invited a father to give a simple talk about his job with the symphony orchestra and play child-friendly tunes on his trombone.

Small or at-home centers can be diverse, too. What if you are a staff of one or just a few? Encourage diversity in your visuals, recordings, and volunteers. Contact a variety of organizations and religious institutions about volunteering at your center. Some major corporations give employees time off from work for volunteer pursuits.

Hiring a Diverse Staff

Making the commitment to a diverse staff is easier than finding and hiring one. It's common not to know many people outside your own group. That makes it challenging to know how to find qualified teachers and assistants who are different from you. Listed are some resources you may not have tapped before:

Houses of worship or other religious institutions can be a great place to recruit loving, consistent people who enjoy young children. Call the minister or other religious leader, or meet people on their turf by going to a service. Let them know the qualifications of the staff you seek. Word will spread of your interest, and people will appreciate that you took time to get to know their culture a little bit.

When you visit an institution that isn't part of your culture, you'll probably be uncomfortable. Go into the experience looking for things you can connect with — food, music, clothing, love of family, or anything else that's important to you. Take along a friend.

Ask community leaders for help. Determine who the leaders are in your target group — be it Hispanic, African-American, Jewish, or something else — and seek out their recommendations for potential staff members. In my town, for instance, I would call the Spanish storyteller at the public library to see if she knows others from her culture who enjoy working with children.

Contact community colleges. Talk with teachers or department heads about promising students in their early childhood programs.

Contact high schools. Ask about successful graduates from home economics and related classes.

Contact senior groups. Don't forget retired people as a rich source of either staff or volunteers. They'll bring a new dimension of experience to your program.

Ask current staff for ideas on finding diverse colleagues.

Advertise jobs in specialty newspapers that your target group reads. You might also research costs for advertising on Spanish-language or other radio stations. Though radio advertising costs might be prohibitive for your center alone, perhaps you can share costs for one ad with several other centers.

In some communities, transportation may be a problem. If you want a highly desirable staff member who lacks reliable transportation, look into whether government agencies provide special bus services, or help arrange a car pool.

Retaining Diverse Staff

Open and honest communication between the director and staff is essential for retaining high-quality personnel. Let staff members know you are committed to supporting them in their work. Make yourself aware of diverse perspectives. Your supportive attitude will make all staff members less likely to leave for other jobs.

Involve staff members in creating the curriculum. Use their cultures as jumping-off points for fun themes. Avoid one-time 'named' celebrations such as Black History Month, which inadvertently communicate that the topic isn't worth studying the rest of the year. Instead, do weekly themes or other small units, weaving diversity into your curriculum all year long. Be creative with holidays. On Presidents' Day, for example, you might bring in several presidents from diverse local organizations. They can tell children what they do and be honored at a party.

Encourage the staff to get to know each other. Have an open house a half-hour before each staff meeting, with refreshments. Invite staffers to come early to relax and talk before the meeting begins.

Consider age-level meetings for teachers. If your center is big, consider paying for a simple dinner mid-year for teachers of twos, then threes, then fours. Teachers could talk about what's been particularly successful for them in activities and themes, and analyze what hasn't worked.

Take your grievance policy seriously. Your grievance policy should be discussed with staff and acted upon when necessary so teachers know it isn't there just for show. It's important that you establish yourself as someone who will listen to grievances. If you follow all the points we've discussed earlier, staff members will trust you and feel free to share information they might not otherwise.

Remember your board. If your center is non-profit, a diverse board can provide a plethora of ideas. It will also demonstrate to staffers that you take diversity seriously.

Banish jokes that are demeaning (based on race, religion, or personal characteristics). It's not political correctness; it's just courtesy.

The more you and your board know about diverse cultures, the easier it will be to retain not only diverse staff members but diverse families. Talk with your board and staff about the ideas in this article, and identify methods that would work for you.

Realize that it's okay to take it slow, a step at a time. At Anne Jones' center, for instance, the board has realized that its small size — 65 families — and fine reputation means there's always a waiting list, filled with the friends of children already at the center. To increase diversity, the center is looking at funding possibilities so that certain slots could be reserved for minority children, possibly on scholarship. The center also plans to advertise in its local African-American newspaper.

"We want to make the effort, because our children are missing an important life experience," Jones says. "Children are very receptive to accepting people for who they are. If they grow up with people who are different from themselves, their neighborhood, or their community, they learn to make decisions about people based on qualities that matter, rather than appearances."

Dream, dream, this is my dream
for the children of the world.
Peace, joy, and happiness
for every boy and girl.
A world where they can play
all in their own way.
A world where they can laugh and cry
and think and wonder why.
A world where there is food to eat,
a home for everyone,
with health and safety a major concern
and schools for them to learn.
A world that holds their children dear
and loves them as they are.
Where children have the chance to grow
and reach a shining star.

— "A Dream for Children"
by Drs. Jan McCarthy and Thomas Moore,
from the recording "Songs for the Whole Day"

Thomas Moore

Dr. Thomas Moore is an early childhood consultant based in Charlotte, North Carolina. He is a nationally recognized keynote speaker and workshop leader and author of *Where is Thumbkin?*, a resource book for teachers. A well-known children's recording artist, his recordings include "I Am Special Just Because I'm Me," "Singing, Moving, & Learning," and "Songs for the Whole Day."

DEVELOPING PEOPLE
IN EARLY CHILDHOOD ORGANIZATIONS

2 CHAPTER 2
Training Staff

Helping Adults Succeed *by Gigi Schweikert* 44

Intentional and Embedded Professional Development *by Sandra Duncan* 48

Creating Environments Where Teachers, Like Children,
Learn Through Play *by Elizabeth Jones* 53

Creative Staff Training is Key to Quality *by Karen Stephens* 58

Principles and Strategies for Coaching and Mentoring *by Margie Carter* 63

Mentors as Teachers, Learners, and Leaders *by Marcy Whitebook and Dan Bellm* 69

The Spirit of Adult Play *by Bonnie Neugebauer* 75

Helping Adults Succeed

Overcoming Barriers to Better Performance

by Gigi Schweikert

As a supervisor, you're probably full of ideas and energy, a strong work ethic, and lots of enthusiasm. So are you wondering why everyone you supervise isn't as excited as you? Do you get frustrated because some adults don't complete the work you ask them to do? One of the greatest challenges for supervisors is realizing that our employees don't always share our expertise and commitment. Sometimes adults do their job and sometimes they don't. And even if our employees do follow through, they often don't do the work like we want it done.

So how do we help adults succeed? Let's think about working with children. If a child isn't functioning well in our program, perhaps having separation problems or misbehaving, we don't immediately say, "What's wrong with that kid?" No, we look at ourselves, we look at our role as a teacher: Did I set up the room appropriately? Are my expectations realistic? Have I given the child enough attention and support? It's the same with adults.

Now let's think about the child who exhibits challenging behavior. As early childhood professionals, we would never say, "I don't think that kid's ever going to crawl, so don't worry about taking that one out of the bouncy seat." We would never work with a preschooler and say, "I don't think that kid will ever learn to read. He doesn't need books." Never!

As teachers, we would never give up on children. We love children and we'd do anything to help them succeed. If we have a child who doesn't want to participate in an art project, but he likes cars, we do crazy, creative things such as, "Let's roll cars through paint." But how often do we give up on adults?

For children, we spend a great deal of energy and creativity to develop an individual care and education plan, create an environment and experience that fits the child, and investigate and use other resources so every child can succeed. Our efforts are endless. But when it comes to the adults, do we think the same way? Usually not. Usually, we expect adults to know what to do when we hire them; and with limited hours of orientation, those adults are on their own. And then, when those same adults fail, that's when we give them plenty of our time, energy, and judgment. Let's help adults, just as we help children, before they fail. That's our job as supervisors.

Help Adults to Succeed, Don't Wait Until They Fail

There aren't many people who wake up in the morning and say, "Today I am going to really mess up at work. First, I'll be late, then not watch the kids, and after that forget to turn in my paperwork." Absolutely not! Adults, like children, don't want to fail. Most of our employees work hard to seek the approval and affirmation of others, the acceptance of and belonging of a group, and the feeling of a job done well. Unfortunately, there are adults who may feel like failures or even losers. Your greatest role as a supervisor is to help adults be successful, to coach them, to teach them, to role-model for them, just like you would do for any child. If you're a master teacher, you have many of the skills to be a master supervisor.

Have Realistic Expectations of Adults

We have to realize, even as supervisors, that we cannot control those around us. We can try to motivate others to perform and control our responses when they don't. Here's the situation. You are good at your job. You get things done. But no matter how good you are, you must depend on the performance of others for your program to function well. There is no way, no matter how good you are, that you could run your center alone. Every single person on your team is important. That's why you have to build on the success of every adult. And here's the deal with most supervisors: You may be an overachiever. Do you have unrealistic expectations of others?

Practice DAP for Adults

As supervisors, we need to remember that some of the people whom we supervise may not perform or aspire to perform as we do, and that's okay. Our expectations as supervisors should be that each employee does her job at an acceptable level of competence, according to what we have asked. Are you expecting your staff to be exactly like you? If you are, then your expectations are unrealistic. So part of helping adults to succeed is setting clear and appropriate expectations. Think about this. You know what DAP is, right? Developmentally Appropriate Practice. Do you use DAP for adults or do you just expect people to be just like you, on your skill level, with the same experience? Can you see the strengths and successes of everyone you supervise and help them perform even better? Do you accept your employees where they are and guide them to learn and grow? You should.

Help Adults Succeed:

■ Appreciate the skills, talents, experience, and ambition of those you supervise.

■ Build on the skills and talents of each employee.

■ Never assume your employees know what you want them to do.

■ Make your expectations simple and specific.

■ Communicate your expectations in a variety of ways — verbal meeting, written statement.

■ Clarify expectations. Ask the employee to tell you what he believes you expect.

■ Address safety issues first when communicating expectations.

■ Focus on one job goal that is not being met or where performance is marginal.

Communicate Clear Expectations:

■ During the interview

■ At the point of hire

■ During orientation

■ In job descriptions

■ On center charts

■ During one-on-one meetings

■ During staff meetings

■ At performance appraisals

■ As an issue arises, but not around the children

Overcome Barriers to Success

Supervisors get frustrated when employees don't perform what to us seems like a simple task. We think, "Shouldn't they just know that?" "Shouldn't they just do that?" Not unless we have told them. But what if we have given the employee simple, clear expectations and the job is still not getting done? What if we ask the employee about a job expectation that is not being accomplished and we are met with reasons or perhaps excuses? I call these 'barriers.' These barriers are real or perceived reasons the employee feels are keeping her from being successful.

Even though an employee may know and understand what she is supposed to do, the employee may feel she can't perform her role because of these barriers. It may sound like this:

Supervisor: "Please make sure you take out the trash after lunch."

Employee: "We don't have enough staff for me to leave the room" (or I don't have enough time before my break).

Some of the barriers that employees state are legitimate, others may be inaccurate perceptions. Although perceptions are certainly their reality, others may be excuses. Don't assume that your employee is making an excuse before you explore the situation.

Let's take a closer look at some of these barriers. Barriers can include time; coverage; limited materials; lack of experience, skills, or confidence; and fear of failure or lack of motivation. Your job as a supervisor is to actively listen to the barriers the employee identifies and then help her eliminate or overcome those barriers. Some people are barrier-spotters; but you, as a supervisor, have to be a barrier-jumper. How am I going to help this person get over this barrier?

Eliminate Barriers:

- Give employees choices
- Solve the barrier issue as a team
- Provide advice based on experience
- Have the person attend a workshop
- Role-model how to overcome the barrier
- Provide encouragement
- Give praise
- Offer your time as a supervisor
- Create a culture that allows employees to question authority

Build Relationships:

- Offer employees choices regarding how they carry out or perform their jobs:
  - "We need a bulletin board for Week of the Young Child. What would you like to do?"
  - "Teachers are bunching up in a group and chatting on the playground when they should be watching the children. How can we make sure all the children are being supervised outside?"
- Give one-on-one attention to each employee through weekly meetings, working alongside the person in the classroom, taking the employee out to lunch, or talking on the phone about how the day went.
- Listen carefully and respond to the employee's real and perceived barriers:
  - "So what I understand from you is that you can't use the water table more often because the children get wet and don't have a change of clothes. Let's send out a note to parents to bring in extra clothes."

- Recognize the importance of being patient and helpful while adults are learning.

- Encourage staff to seek help from each other:

  - "Dana, in Toddler Room 2, has a lot of good ideas for helping with transition. I can arrange for you to spend some time in her room."

- Understand the intensity of feelings regarding change:

  - "Having family-style meals with children is messy and much harder than on the adults serving it. Why don't you just start with snack?"

- Intervene and help the employee before she is too frustrated or overwhelmed:

  - "Let me help you get the children dressed to go outside."

- Provide a culture that allows for venting. Listen to the employee, repeat to see if you understand her feelings, and then help her deal with the issue.

  - "It sounds like that parent could have spoken to you more politely. I'm sorry. I'll speak with the parent, but in the meantime we need to think of a way to make sure all of her child's things are ready to go at the end of the day. How can we do that?"

Here's the Deal

How do we help adults succeed? Just as we would with children: Accept everyone where they are. Then we can determine how to help that adult become a better early childhood professional. That's it? That's it. And it doesn't happen overnight. And some employees may never reach your level of expertise, nor do they want to. That's okay, too. Most importantly, never give up on an adult. You'd never do that to a child.

Gigi Schweikert

Gigi Schweikert is the working mother of four children and author of 18 books on parenting and early childhood education, including the best-selling *Winning Ways series* with Redleaf Press. With 25 years' experience, Gigi's practical ideas and realistic perspective on child care will have you laughing and learning. Gigi's an international keynote speaker, recently in Malaysia and New Zealand, and she'd love to come to your program, no matter where you are. She's on the advisory board of KidReports and believes technology can keep us connected.

Intentional and Embedded Professional Development

Four Steps to Success

by Sandra Duncan

Recently, much attention has been focused on the importance of intentionality when working with and teaching young children. Intentional teachers "act purposefully with a goal in mind and a plan to accomplish it" (Epstein, 2007, p. 4). In the intentional classroom, there is a synergistic partnership between the children and teacher. Although the teacher is actively involved in creating supportive environments and learning experiences, children in an intentional classroom also play an active role in the learning process. There is a purposeful balance between child-guided and adult-guided experiences. This balance is accomplished through a variety of teaching strategies that best encourages each child's development and acquisition of knowledge. Just as our profession is becoming more purposeful and intentional about choosing the best strategies for promoting children's learning and development, so should we exercise the same level of intentionality when creating professional development programs for early childhood practitioners.

Intentional Professional Development

In order to be intentional about professional development, it is important to design training programs that reflect what we know about adult learning. Much of what we know about adult learning mirrors what is known about best practices in children's learning. For example, both child and adult learning is most effective when:

- learners actively participate in relevant and meaningful experiences.

- new knowledge is constructed from current knowledge.

- there is sufficient time given for practicing new skills.

- opportunities are provided for reflection (Knowles, 1973; Sparks, 1994; Wolfe, 2001).

There are four key steps to creating a successful and intentional professional development program.

Step 1:
Understanding Staff Needs

Early childhood teachers use authentic observations and informal assessments of children to inform their curriculum planning. Through listening and observing, effective teachers understand children's needs and interests so they are able to plan experiences and activities that are relevant and meaningful. Likewise, directors and/or trainers should also gather staff

Levels of Professional Growth and Possible Survey Questions

Professional Growth Level	Challenges of Level	Possible Survey Questions
#1: Survival	• Surviving Daily Routines and Transitions • Improving Classroom Management	• What are your challenges in child guidance? • Where could you use some help in classroom management?
#2: Consolidation	• Increasing Knowledge Base • Strengthening Specific Skills	• What intrigues you about child growth and development? • What specific skills are important for you to learn?
#3: Renewal	• Decreasing Personal Enthusiasm • Gaining New Ideas	• What topics of interest would you like to explore in more depth? • Are there new teaching approaches or strategies that you would like to learn?
#4: Maturity	• Enhanced Professional Growth • Search for Insight and Increased Responsibilities	• Are you interested in helping others with professional development and in what way? • In what areas do you feel most competent? Can you think of ways to share your knowledge?

information to help inform the development of staff training. A survey or needs assessment is one way to gather this type of information.

In writing the survey, it is important to include questions that address the needs of the entire staff. This is challenging because there is no typical staff — each staff's composition is unique with diverse teaching experiences and varied educational backgrounds and individuals who are operating at different levels of professional development. One way to address this challenge is to consider Lilian Katz's (1972) four levels of professional growth — survival, consolidation, renewal, and maturity — since there are different training needs associated with each level of growth. For example, a teacher who is in the survival stage may be more interested in training that involves learning about day-to-day routines or managing children's behavior while a mature teacher may be looking for new ideas, teaching strategies, and increased responsibilities or challenges. Be sure to include questions that would address the needs

of each level of professional growth; this will inform your training program's objectives and learning experiences.

Another way to determine staff needs is to have informal conversations or brown bag lunches for small groups of teachers. This idea is especially effective if you explain Katz's four levels of professional development, ask teachers to determine their level, and intentionally plan conversations that meet the needs of a particular level of professional growth.

Step 2:
Engaging Teachers in the Planning Process

As early childhood practitioners, we understand the importance of children's choice or self-initiated activity. A child-initiated experience is "an activity wholly decided on by the child and is the result of an intrinsic motivation to explore a project or express an idea. In doing this the child may use a variety of resources and demonstrate a complex range of knowledge, skills, and understanding" (Qualifications and Curriculum Authority, 2008, p. 9). When children initiate exploration, they express more interest and increased motivation to learn through their experiences.

Similarly, research on staff development suggests that teachers are more actively involved and committed to learning when they are engaged in the planning process (Hanover Research Council, 2008). Research also suggests that aligning the program's training objectives to learners' needs or challenges, interests, and levels of expertise and/or knowledge is an effective strategy for developing staff training programs (Chen & Chang, 2006). Being actively involved in the planning process means that teachers are given opportunities to decide what they want to know, why it is important to them, and where and how they will acquire the knowledge. This approach is similar to the classroom K-W-L Approach where teachers find out what children know, what they want to know, and finally what they have learned.

The K-W-L Approach provides a course of action for creating professional development programs based on the teacher's interest, acquired knowledge, and pedagogy. This approach can also be used as a way of engaging teachers in the planning process. After discovering topics of interest and/or problematic areas through a survey, needs assessment, or informal conversations, the director and/or trainer leads a discussion with an individual or a small group of teachers who have expressed interest in similar topics and are operating at the same level of professional growth. This discussion focuses on what the teachers know and what they want to know. Also decided is how and where learning will occur, such as attending conferences, reading books, researching the Internet, enrolling in a university course, partnering with a mentor, and/or observing and interacting with others. To ensure accountability, the learner and trainer/director should be jointly agreed upon: 1) learning objectives and goals, 2) timeline, and 3) receivables such as portfolio, journal, artifact,

presentation, photograph, and/or evidence of teacher reflection.

Step 3:
Practicing New Knowledge

As early childhood educators, we believe that children best construct knowledge through self-initiated active interactions with the environment. We also know that children need time to practice their language, theories, and relationships. Likewise, research suggests teachers learn best through active involvement in the classroom environment. An effective strategy of professional development is training that is embedded into the teacher's day in the classroom (Sparks, 1997). Job-embedded training should directly connect to the K-W-L Approach so classroom learning experiences are intentional and goal-driven. As with children, teachers need adequate time to practice new skills. Job-embedded training should not be a one-time, isolated experience. Rather, it should be viewed as continuous and ongoing by encouraging teachers to view their daily experiences with children as opportunities to learn. The K-W-L chart, therefore, should be a living document for each teacher.

Step 4:
Reflecting on Experiences

According to Dewey (1933), reflecting on one's experiences is as important as the experience itself. Much can be learned by taking a reflective perspective. Reflection "helps teachers make meaningful conclusions and observations about their teaching practices which, in turn, shapes and molds their behavior" (Duncan, 2008, p. 4). But, in order to be effective, reflection must be intentionally embedded into the professional development program — which brings us to the final step in the K-W-L Approach. Reflecting on classroom experiences encourages teachers to consider relationships, underlying causes, and assumptions. In the finicky eater situation, the

K-W-L CHART

Teacher:_____Miss Smith_____

Professional Growth Level:_____Consolidation_____

Topic of Interest:_____Finicky Eaters_____

What Teacher Knows	What Teacher Wants to Learn	What Teacher Learned (Reflection)
Several children will not eat their vegetables at lunch.

Children need to eat a variety of foods to be healthy. | How to get children to eat a well-balanced meal.

How to encourage children to try new foods, including eating their vegetables. | • I learned how to introduce new foods to children by using a three step method of 1) introduce, 2) investigate, and 3) intake.
• I learned that children are more apt to eat their vegetables when they are involved in the preparation.
• I learned there is a strong connection between children's eating habits and their family, so parenting education is important. |

teacher learned that families also influence children's eagerness to try new foods. Through reflection, the teacher was able to assess the situation and make intentional decisions on ways to encourage children to eat vegetables at lunch.

Conclusion

Successful professional development can only be achieved when the learner is intentionally engaged in the learning process. When teachers are given opportunities to help determine their training curriculum and educational path, they become more invested, involved, and committed to the learning process.

References

Chen, J., & Chang, C. (2006, Spring). "Testing the whole teacher approach to professional development: A study of enhancing early childhood teachers' technology proficiency." *Early Childhood Research & Practice*, (8)1.

Dewey, J. (1933). *How we think*. Boston: D.C. Heath.

Duncan, S. (2008, Fall). "Which is better: Staff recruitment or staff retention?" *Professional Connections, 1-5*, 11.

Epstein, A. (2007). *The intentional teacher: Choosing the best strategies for young children's learning*. Washington, DC: NAEYC.

Hanover Research Council. (2008). *The exemplary staff development model*. Washington, DC: Author.

Katz, L. (1972). "The developmental stages of preschool teachers." *Elementary School Journal, 73*(1), 50-54.

Knowles, M. (1973). *The adult learner: A neglected species*. Houston: Gulf Publishing Company.

Loucks-Horsley, S., Harding, D., Arbuckle, M., Dubeau, C., Williams, M., & Murray, L. (1987). *Continuing to learn: A guidebook for teacher development*. Oxford, OH: The National Staff Development Council and the Regional Laboratory for Educational Improvement of the Northeast and Islands.

Qualifications and Curriculum Authority (QCA). (2008). *Early years foundation stage profile handbook*. London: Author.

Sparks, D. (1994). "A paradigm shift in staff development." *Journal of Staff Development, 15*(4), 26-30.

Sparks, D., & Hirsh, S. (1997). *A new vision for staff development*. Alexandria, VA: Association for Supervision and Curriculum Development.

Wolfe, P. (2001). *Brain matters: Translating research into classroom practice*. Alexandria, VA: Association for Supervision and Curriculum Development.

Sandra Duncan

As adjunct faculty, Sandra Duncan works with doctoral candidates at Nova Southeastern University Fischler Graduate School of Education and teaches early childhood education at Ivy Tech Community College. She is the co-author of *Inspiring Spaces for Young Children* and *Rating Observation Scale for Young Children*. Proud grandma of preschooler Sierra Elizabeth, she can be reached at sandrdun@aol.com.

Creating Environments Where Teachers, Like Children, Learn Through Play

by Elizabeth Jones

People who are concerned with providing good environments for young children are often very clear about what young children's needs for learning are. They really believe children learn through play, through making changes in a rich environment. They go to a whole lot of trouble to set up such environments for children.

Administrators of programs for young children, especially if they have been teachers previously, tend to focus on the learning needs of the children and to overlook these same needs in the adults they supervise. I learned this from my friend Chris Morgan, who as director of a children's center in Hayward, California, came to the realization that "my responsibility is to the adults in this setting. If I make a good learning environment for them, then they'll make a good learning environment for the children. The adults are the people I have to set up the environment for."

Administrators really need to think of the needs of adults in much the same terms in which they, as teachers, thought of the needs of children. Adults need to be safe, they need to have enough resources to work with, and they need to be encouraged to play.

Playful Learning

When a child is learning through play she gets to explore — there isn't a predetermined end product. She has an idea or notion of a direction she would like to pursue and she is free within broad limits to do so. Her motivation comes from within herself as she interacts with the possibilities in the environment.

Administrators responsible for training staff often find themselves trying to motivate the staff members to learn what has been predetermined that they must learn. But if you want people to stay excited about their jobs, there has to be some opportunity for them to explore, to be decision makers, to say, "This is what I want to do next." That's playful in the very best sense. Children become active learners through play; and so do adults.

My friend Dave Riley, a California consultant, has implemented this concept through a consultation model, which I believe could be used by administrators as well. What he mostly did was to come in as an observer. He would spend the day seeing what was going on, writing detailed factual notes, and sharing these with the teachers at the end of the day. This sharing immediately raised their questions and comments. Then he'd ask questions like: "What things do you like that you are doing? What things don't you like that you would like to work on? What's your next strategy for any problem you're having that you want to deal with?"

If teachers were having trouble inventing strategies and solutions and asked for help, Dave often relied upon storytelling. He had hundreds of stories in his head, based on teaching situations he had observed. He used these to describe how other teachers handled similar problems. He deliberately presented them as examples, not as prescriptions. It was up to the teachers to find something in the experiences of others to hook onto and decide, "Oh, if that's the case, then maybe if I tried this, this would happen."

At the end of each session Dave would ask the teacher to make a commitment to work on her strategy before their next session. This underscored the importance of the decision-making process by which the teachers decided what it was they cared about and what they wanted to do about it.

This consulting model is a good example of a basic approach to working with adults. The trainer says to the trainee, "What do you want to do? How do you want to go about it? What resources do you need from me? When shall we talk about it again?" And then at the following meeting, "What did you do? How did it work?" This is a continual planning and evaluation process with the initiative coming from the trainee. The trainer assumes the role of a mentor in this process. He is saying, "Hey, I really think you are competent and I'm prepared to help you do what you are committed to doing."

Closed Means — Open Ends

This playful approach will not work the same for all teachers, and for some it may not work at all. Many teachers, especially newer ones, will get stuck way back at the question: "What do you want to do?" Bill Baker, Early Childhood Coordinator for Alameda County (CA) Schools, taught me a useful approach to this problem when he was on the Pacific Oaks

faculty. He describes learning situations as involving both ends (where you're going), and means (how you're getting there). Means and ends can be either closed or open. You can have closed means and closed ends, closed means and open ends, open means and open ends, or open means and closed ends. Each combination has a different effect on the learning process.

Many tasks for learners involve **closed means and closed ends**, where both the goal for learning and the procedure for learning it are carefully prescribed in advance. "Learn this material in order to pass the test"; "Teach this lesson in this way and we will evaluate what happened." This approach is useful as a way of letting people check out their competence at something, but it has disadvantages as a learning process. The trouble with many such tasks is that either people can't do them very well or else they don't fit in well with where people are at.

Tasks of this sort become unenjoyable labor. Where teachers spend most of their time at such tasks, they are likely to develop the attitude "What do I have to do to satisfy that person over there — the enemy?" instead of taking responsibility for their own work.

Not only does the closed means/closed ends approach inhibit motivation, it is also often ineffective in terms of results. You can teach a lot of information, which adults can pick up and say and do partly. But all of us learn so selectively that a supposedly efficient closed means/closed-ends process is unlikely to be effective in teacher training. While you're telling someone how to do something, there will be 25 other things going on in that person's head. An individual has got to do his own sequencing and make his own connections. He will only hear as much of what you say to him as he can do something with.

I have had much more success in using **closed means/open ends** tasks to get people started. I give directions that are very specific: "Go find a partner and tell her six things about yourself." So it's very explicit as to what they are supposed to do, but what comes out of it is wide open. It's not "Go find a partner and work out answers to these five math problems." There's permission to open once you've gotten started.

As an administrator with a new teacher, you might say, "Today, go mix three colors of paint, put them out on the easel, and see what the children can do with them." The task starts closed, but it gives teachers a chance to begin plugging in their own curiosity and their own questions. Essentially you are trying to get the play process started, for both children and teacher.

If you are experienced at all, you will have some notion of what you want teachers to learn most quickly. Once you have selected a starting point, you let teachers make their own choices as to where they want to go with it. You are not giving up on quality standards for programs by allowing people to make their own choices. You are simply trying to legitimize the sequence of choices this individual wants to make. Once you've done this, you don't have to worry about motivation. Most people, including grown-ups, will make good choices for themselves if they are really trusted, supported, and given enough time. The only point at which you would intervene is when an individual gets stuck or is persistently not making choices that you see as essential. You are always free as the trainer to say, "It's my turn. Today I'm going to tell you what to do."

For example, you may have a teacher whose communication skills leave a great deal to be desired and who isn't choosing that direction to work on. At some point you might say "Look, I think you're ready to work on a goal I'd like to set for you and these are some ways I'd like you to go about it." You then have to decide whether or not you are giving this person a choice or making a non-negotiable demand. In extreme cases you might even have to say, "If you're not ready to work on this, I'm going to recommend that you be fired."

Mae Varon, a preschool teacher here at Pacific Oaks, has used a related approach in helping her practicum students set goals for themselves. At the beginning of one semester she listed 10 possible goals and asked students to add two of their own. She then had them prioritize these 12 goals for themselves. She provided quite a bit of pre-structure; she didn't ask them to invent a dozen goals. However, the ones that students put at the top of their lists were up to them. Then she said, "You can work on the top three on your list — for this semester, ignore the rest." In effect she was saying "Pick a manageable number of goals for yourself and I will hold you accountable for them."

The Inquiry Model

A friend of mine, teaching child development, was trying to figure out how to teach Freudian theory. It occurred to her to ask the class what they knew about it. They knew quite a lot; some of it accurate, some of it not. But by the time they had it all down, the class had an experience base to build from.

As an administrator you can do the same thing; you can assume that the adults are competent. There is, in fact, quite a lot of competence there, and some will be self-fulfilling if you assume it's there.

When confronting a new issue or problem, for example, you may want to start with the staff. You will eventually, as a group, start asking quite specific questions. At this point you could bring in an expert to supply specific answers, if that's what's needed.

But I don't think you bring in experts until you've got questions for them. It's a real drag to have experts come in telling you things all the time. While you're supposed to be listening, you're doing your shopping list in your head because the question wasn't one you had asked. You should only bring someone in after you, as a staff, have already established yourselves as knowledgeable. Then afterwards you can argue about whether the expert was right. (The demythologizing of outside experts is probably a useful thing for staff to experience.)

You want people who are working with children to be decision makers and to feel competent about their own role. I think you add expertise in little increments as people say, "I want to know these specific things."

To be this kind of administrator, you ask questions more than you give answers. You employ an inquiry model. You keep asking, "What do you think? Why do you think this way? What are you going to do about it?"

You don't behave this way at all unless you trust the latent potential of your staff. If you are basically convinced they are unknowledgeable and unmotivated and that you are the authority, then this approach will never work.

Open Communication Channels

To support learning in your center, it helps to set up a very clear communication structure so that you keep getting feedback. When I lead groups I always try to get some written, as well as oral, feedback. In my classes I often communicate back and forth with students through folders. (Each student has a folder, kept in an accessible place.) I may take time and ask, "What worked well for you today? What didn't you like? Take 10 minutes and write it down." Then I write responses to their comments in their folders.

I know of administrators who have done this as well. One told me, "I tried this and it really worked. They really did write." Each staff member had a folder in the office. No one was required to write so many words per day, but they were guaranteed a response from the administrator every time they wrote anything.

The reason for encouraging such writing is that it offers one more chance to communicate. In centers, teachers and administrators are often so busy that their schedules don't allow frequent opportunities for face-to-face contact. When a teacher has something she wants to tell the administrator and knows

she won't catch her today, one thing she can do is to write a note. You don't do this instead of face-to-face contacts, you do it in addition.

You are trying to build a very lively communications network. Sometimes you give very explicit tasks: "Write down what your goals are for yourself and prioritize them. Then we'll talk about them." Sometimes you ask staff simply to relate incidents: "Please tell me the best and the worst things that happened this week." To be a good administrator you have to know a lot about what's going on, and this is one more way of ensuring that you do.

Written staff communication adds a new dimension to the administrator's job and administrators who don't like to write probably can't do it. Some teachers will not want to write, and that needs to be okay. Also, in a very small center (with a staff of three or so) you probably need not bother with writing. But by the time a center gets up to a dozen people you're not going to be able to talk to everybody, and written communications become more important.

Peer Supports

I would be very inclined as an administrator to try to build peer groups, to make people accountable to their peers as to how they are expending their time, and not just to the administrator. You want to give people all the opportunities you can to be supports and communicators for each other. Among other reasons, that relieves you of a lot of responsibility. If people are supporting each other, you won't have to do it all as the administrator. Furthermore, it will always happen that there is somebody on the staff who can support someone else better than you can. There will also be staff members who know more about certain problems than you do; everyone benefits if you make use of their knowledge.

It is not enough to say, "We are all resources for each other." You have to structure so that it will happen. You might do networking on what people's goals are. In a staff meeting you could go around the room and ask everyone as specific a question as possible about their work toward their goals. For example: "What have you done in the past week to accomplish your goal to learn how to do music with children?" With this structure staff are free to choose their own goals and decide how to accomplish them, but they can't do it privately. They have to be accountable to their peers by saying in effect, "I'm being a responsible team member and these are the things I'm doing."

Another way to encourage communication networks is to have written communications be not just between staff and the director, but among everybody. In my classes, for example, folders are open to everyone. (Particular notes can be marked confidential if desired.) Students are free to read others' folders and to make comments on them. Initially they often have trouble with this openness; they feel as if they are eavesdropping. But eventually we get all sorts of complicated conversations going in the folders, with notes upon notes in the margin.

I've also seen a 'complaints/compliments' approach to children's communication work well in an elementary school setting. To apply this method at the center level, an administrator could ask each staff member to write a complaint to somebody and a compliment to somebody else and to put these in their folders.

In whatever structuring you do, you need to be sensitive to how different staff members will react. If the teacher aides are intimidated by the head teachers, you may find it works best to have the aides meet separately for these types of activities. If people are reluctant to open up in large groups, you make a point of dividing into smaller and smaller groups (down to pairs, if necessary) until communication is flowing.

You can also structure with the tasks you assign. If you ask nice big intellectual questions, the most sophisticated people in the group will dominate the discussion. If you don't want that to happen you might narrow the focus by asking, for example, "What happened to you yesterday with a child that

you didn't understand?" If you want everybody to talk in a discussion, you must structure so that it will happen. Generally you will want to tighten up to make things happen at the outset, then loosen up as communications start to flow.

Typically these types of activities generate all kinds of interactions. People end up sharing professional problems and giving and receiving all kinds of advice. It's sort of a mutual growth process. You want to build enough levels of communication among staff so that they know each other well and care about what happens to each other. If they feel safe together, if they are resources for each other, then they will be able to take the risks involved in playful learning. Adults do learn through play; and where they are learning, children are likely to be learning, too.

Elizabeth Jones

Elizabeth Jones, Ph.D., is a faculty member at Pacific Oaks College in Pasadena, California, and co-author of several publications including, *The "Politics" of Day Care* and *Supporting the Growth of Infants, Toddlers, and Parents.*

Creative Staff Training is Key to Quality

by Karen Stephens

Director to director, let's talk turkey about program quality. No matter how spiffy and chic our child care center building may look, no matter how high-techy we're able to equip and supply classrooms, and no matter how much money we can spend for public relations and advertising promotions — a program's quality is determined by staff attitude and performance — first, last, and always.

Staff are the most valuable, and temperamental, of program assets. Whether interacting with children, parents, or each other, how well staff meets its job challenges ultimately makes or breaks a program's image and reputation. Our programs are only as good as the staff we're able to hire, retain, support, and consistently motivate to high performance.

Without the strong foundation of wise, committed staff that possess professional skills, program quality quickly slips down a slippery slope. Even our newly-built, avant-garde child care buildings will be little more than warehouses. Void of energized and talented staff, any building is merely a shell where potential for engaging childhoods evaporates into thin air. In the wake are left hollow memories — not sustaining, life affirming ones. That abysmal picture shortchanges children and families, and most certainly robs the future of a stable society.

Today's status quo of working conditions, wages, and benefits in child care means that keeping a good staff is a continual challenge. But we can't let that distract us from investing in the staff we DO have. The best investment programs ensure staff is consistently — and creatively — trained so they'll continue to be fascinated by their work with children.

There are a variety of ways to keep staff in step with skilled professional practice, such as funding conference or workshop attendance. Some programs subsidize costs for continuing formal education, often by obtaining corporate/foundation grants or participating in government quality enhancement initiatives. Some directors can even build budgets that include an on-site consultant for individualized, ongoing training support.

Considering resources, there are still a lot of directors who have no choice but to provide training themselves. For typical topics, like child abuse reporting procedures, that's fine. But if your training involves asking staff to change or try new ideas, it's hard to be a prophet in your own land. To enhance training vitality and variety, experienced directors often swap training responsibilities for their respective staff — a bartering system, so to speak. It you make the right match, it works.

However you arrange it, training must be a priority for every program, regardless of how programs vary in terms of staff turnover and staff qualifications. Through training you'll help your staff maintain their resilient, good hearts and also develop their keen minds.

With that said, the following are steps to make staff training well-targeted, creative, and useful. When training proves successful, the staff's work life becomes more enriching and satisfying. And to be sure, well-trained staff greatly increases the odds that your child care building will be filled with the joy of cherished childhood memories in the making. Bottom line, that's what program quality should be about.

Identify Training Needs:

■ Select training topics based on job descriptions, as well as current staff experience and qualifications. Training will impact staff performance most when it is tailored to members' current needs. A new, inexperienced staff requires different training than a staff with lots of seniority.

■ Review licensing requirements that stipulate mandatory training topics. Plan topics in response to improvement suggestions from recent licensing visits.

■ Compare program operation with accreditation criteria for high quality. A formal self-study using NAEYC accreditation criteria is very helpful in spotting staff training needs, even if your program doesn't pursue accreditation.

■ To pinpoint training needs, observe staff performance regularly through announced, as well as unannounced, visits. While observing, note exceptionally skilled staff so they can become resources for mentors or peer trainers.

■ Survey staff to find out suggested training topics, preferred methods of training delivery, and best times to hold training. Ask staff what they are excited to learn more about!

■ During evaluations, ask staff to reflect on skills or knowledge that need bolstering. Cooperatively draft a plan for professional development that responds to those needs.

■ Analyze recent parent comments and concerns to reveal training needs. Staff, volunteers, or lab students also make insightful comments that infer training needs.

Select Training Topic and Define Target Audience:

■ Select participants based on the work you did in Step 1. For instance, you might want to offer training on understanding and responding to biting incidents in the toddler room. That would define your target audience as well.

■ Formulate a desired training group size. Tough, touchy, or confidential topics call for a smaller group size. Other topics may involve the whole staff. When all staff are in attendance, break into small groups when possible so more people get a chance to speak. And remember, your group size will influence how you deliver training.

■ Decide who will be required to attend versus who will be invited to attend. Toddler teachers may be required to attend a training on biting; but other staff may appreciate being included — plus they can provide insight. In the case of biting, infant caregivers could give insight on a specific child's development prior to his enrollment in the toddler room. That sharing leads to peer mentoring and team building between classroom assignments.

Define Training Goals:

■ Write down desired performance outcomes that will result from training. Be as specific as you can. A vague, general goal doesn't get you good results. Share your goals with the staff and encourage them to buy into training by identifying their own goals as well.

■ Identify content knowledge and skills staff need to meet desired outcomes. To increase the chances of successful training, break outcomes down into steps that are realistically achievable.

■ Anticipate a timeline for achievement of training goals. Estimate how many training sessions will be needed to ensure staff competence. If you set a timeline, include staff in the process so they can invest energy and commitment. This also helps prevent overwhelming staff with expectations too high for immediate mastery.

Select Methods of Presentation and Activities:

■ Plan and implement training that is as hands-on and interactive as possible. For long-lasting learning, experiential training is absolutely the way to go. Everyone learns best by doing.

■ Whenever possible, interject training with humor. Allow the time and freedom needed for imagination and brainstorming to work its magic. For instance, if you want training to boost staff's creativity quotient, engage them in activities that will require them to practice resourcefulness — whether it is using blocks, art supplies, makeshift music instruments, dramatic play materials, or whatever.

■ Vary training activities based on the time you'll have in each session and how many training sessions the topic needs for thorough coverage. Marathon training sessions can overwhelm and fatigue staff. Processing time is needed for training content to sink in and make sense. If you offer a two-hour session, break it up in the middle with a relevant video or engaging music during which members can snack on refreshments and move around.

■ Plan activities that appeal to a variety of learning styles. Don't limit yourself to lecture or half of your staff will tune out — especially if you train after a long day of work. Following are examples of alternatives to lecture format training:

• Stage a mock magazine news show (like "20/20" or "Dateline") so staff can interview each other on the pros and cons of topics, such as use of computers with young children.

• To explore all angles of a topic, include role-play when possible, such as staff acting out the scenario of a parent arriving after closing time.

• Read to the staff a relevant children's book and use reactions to guide discussion. *The Kissing Hand* by Audrey Penn or *Owl Babies* by Martin Waddel are both great lead-ins to separation anxiety discussions.

• Prior to a meeting, have staff record answers to reflection questions designed to put them in a receptive mindset for training. If training is on nature education, ask staff to reflect on nature adventures they experienced during their childhood and ask them to share them with others.

• Hold a poster session where staff highlight before-and-after photos that relate to the training topic, such as room arrangement, learning center development, or curriculum documentation.

• Post mural paper on training room walls. Have staff web out or list ideas to discuss that relate to the training topic. For instance, toilet training requires staff to consider child development, parent expectations, personal biases, communication with parents, changing table particulars, family cultural beliefs, pros and cons of Pull-ups, and so on. Allow the staff to decide where discussions should begin. They can also identify resource materials and local experts to help them explore the topic.

Provide Good Training Resources for Future Use:

■ No one remembers everything they experience during training. Provide a meeting agenda and outline to refresh memories after training. Folders of resource references also help staff revisit training ideas or explore them more deeply. Provide a video on the training topic that staff can check out when questions arise. Websites to refer to are becoming increasingly popular. And don't forget to identify skilled team mentors whose expertise can be tapped for support.

Evaluate Training:

- Evaluation of training is critical. Both the director and staff should decide if training was worthwhile or a waste of time. Evaluation helps you plan future training events that will be well received and influential on staff performance. Ask staff to give written feedback on training strengths and weaknesses, as well as organization and delivery. Ask them to cite a few concepts, tips, or ideas they picked up that could immediately be put into practice.

- Evaluate training success by observing classrooms to see if practice has changed. Also interview parents and team staff to determine if training made an impact. Don't forget, go right to children and ask them their opinions. Children are incredibly honored to be a focus group.

Finishing Touches:
Infuse Training With Meaning

In today's hurried schedules, everyone's time is so precious. Time spent in training inevitably means staff are losing time with their own families. Recognition of that personal sacrifice, and appreciation for the dedication it confirms, should motivate directors to infuse staff training with as much meaning as possible. Show staff respect by making sure training is worthwhile and valuable. Disrespect is shown if we treat professional development as merely putting in time to meet minimum licensing standards for in-service hours.

- Arrange the training room in anticipation of staff. Have adequate materials set out and ready to use on time.

- Create comfort for a relaxed sense of community and camaraderie. Seating should be comfy and scaled for an adult's body. Room temperature should be cozy — not too cool or too hot. Natural lighting or even mood lighting lifts spirits. Candles add warmth and ambiance, as can simple windchimes or background music. Fresh flowers or a bubbling tabletop fountain contribute beauty and harmony. Such small things are easy to overlook, but they really do show respect — and they make a big difference. Quality is in the details, even ones we often take for granted.

- Nourish the body as well as the mind — provide your staff with food! Refreshments should be tasty and even fun, and always encourage socializing.

- Provide participants with a focus object they can hold and manipulate. The best focus objects symbolize something about the training and its intent. One of my favorites focus object strategies:

  - When training participants arrive, there's a small selection of mirrored pebbles at each seat. As the group gathers, I encourage them to make designs with their pebbles and to show them off to each other. They can keep the pebbles during the training in case they get fidgety.

  - I begin the training session by sharing my personal philosophy of teaching — whether with children or adults. I envision myself as a pebble — a pebble with some knowledge about kids and some experience with them. Whenever I share my insights, I envision my pebbly-self dropped into a pond. I make a ripple that hopefully circles out widely to make a positive impact on all it touches — the training participants and the children in their care in particular.

  - At the end of the training, just before participants leave, I hand each one a mirrored pebble to keep — a talisman if you will, to remind them of what they learned and of our shared commitment to children and families. I tell each person they're a pebble, too, able to share her knowledge with others so life is better for us all.

Yep, I'm a sucker for symbolism and sentiment. Luckily, there are many simple items that can symbolize useful metaphors for our field. Choose symbols that relate well to your specific training topics. Some suggestions:

- A packet of garden seeds or a simple daisy reminds staff to bloom with confidence.

- A tiny container of playdough reminds them to be flexible during times of change; silly putty suggests that humor is a great way to maintain perspective.

- A bottle of bubbles reminds staff to manage stress by taking time to play on their own. (Or if staff are in the habit of complaining, bubbles can remind them to lighten up!)

- A lucky penny reminds staff that an optimistic attitude can help change take place easier.

- A candle sheds light on new opportunities.

You get my meaning. Use your imagination. Trust it to inspire you and you'll come up with a wonderful symbolic token to infuse your training with meaning.

Now, I don't know about you, but I'm going to the hobby store to buy some more mirrored pebbles!

Karen Stephens

Karen Stephens, M.S. in education specializing in early childhood, began her career as a teacher in a preschool classroom in 1975. From 1980 to May 2013 she served as campus child care director and taught child development and early childhood program administration courses for the Illinois State University's Department of Family and Consumer Sciences. Today she writes from her home and enjoys occasional travel to deliver staff development training and conference presentations.

Principles and Strategies for Coaching and Mentoring

by Margie Carter

With the revolving door we face in trying to staff our child care programs, there is a growing desire among directors to learn how to set up coaching and mentoring systems. Ideally, a peer coaching process not only helps newcomers to the field, but enhances the professional development and retention of those who have more expertise. However, given the financial and organizational limitations that typically bind directors, you will probably need to do most of the coaching yourself, at least initially.

To be sure, there are contradictions inherent in having the role of supervisor and coach in one person. The trust, open communication, and mutual respect required for healthy mentoring relationships are difficult to maintain when one party has the power to hire and fire.

For you to be an effective coach, you will need a clear distinction in your mind between evaluating and seeking compliance on the one hand and nurturing a learning process on the other. Understanding the difference between 'telling' and a pedagogy that helps people construct their own understandings and become reflective teachers is central to your ability to enhance quality job performance.

Principle:
Think in terms of a learning and empowerment process

As a director, start with yourself, enhancing your own understandings of adult pedagogy and the empowerment process. Practice your mentoring skills with your most able staff members so that before long you can establish a peer coaching system.

Strategy:
Reflect on the learning process in your own life

One way to begin rethinking your approach to staff development is to identify something new you, yourself, have learned in your adult life. Take a minute to remember how that happened. How did you go about this learning? What motivated you and what barriers did you overcome? Did anyone else have a role in your learning? If so, how did that relationship work? If you learned on your own, what strategies did you use? Now compare this memory to the typical in-service training you offer in your program. How is it similar or different?

Most people's mental image of teacher training is a workshop setting where the director is in front of the room explaining something to the group. Was this your experience in the learning process you remembered in the suggested activity above? Most people say that sitting and listening to someone describe information plays a small role in their learning.

The learning process you described above was probably more involved than that. Perhaps it included such things as experimenting, reading, observing, talking things over with someone, trying out new ideas, making mistakes, perhaps practicing over and over again. Possibly you had a coach or a model that you apprenticed yourself to. Remembering the variety of ways that adults go about learning should help you assess your work with your staff. If your approach to training is limited to 'telling' sessions or workshop formats, you might be missing the boat.

Listed are some additional principles and strategies to guide your thinking.

Principle:
Treat your staff as you would have them treat children

I'm continually surprised at the contradiction between how directors plan and respond to staff and what they want teachers to be doing with the children. Whether or not you have studied adult learning theory, your knowledge of good practices for children can be translated into appropriate practices for educating teachers.

How could you justify anything to the contrary? We have a number of research studies that highlight the link between the quality of the work experience for staff and the quality of care that children receive. The idea of creating an environment and educational activities for adults that parallel what you want them to do with children is not only one of quality and of ethics, but an issue of pedagogy as well. Adults have to experience the value of certain activities and responses to children if they are to understand their significance and incorporate these into their own approach.

Strategy:
List parallel components

Providing adults with experiences that parallel what we want for children should be at the center of a director's thinking. If we want caregivers to offer well-designed and pleasing learning environments for children, we need to design an environment like that for them. If teachers are to give children choices and opportunities for self-initiated learning, then they deserve that from us.

Take out your favorite list of components for quality child care. Use a paper with a vertical line drawn down the middle. On the left side, list the quality components for children; and on the right side opposite each component, write one for the staff. With your staff, prioritize the top three changes you want to make and develop an action plan with a timeline. You'll be amazed by the improved dispositions and performance in your staff.

Principle:
Know your adult learners

Adults bring a complex web of experiences, knowledge, skills, and attitudes to the learning process. They have a developmental process, just as children do. Their own childhoods and their cultural framework have shaped their self-image and how they respond to children and their co-workers. Staff members come to our programs with particular dispositions towards people in positions of authority and different emotional responses to the idea of making changes.

To be effective in staff development, you must take time to discover who your staff members are and, in Carol Ann Wien's words, their "scripts for action." You must recognize what they already know, build on that, and plan training that is relevant and meaningful for their lives. Isn't this just what you hope they will do with the children in their care?

Strategy:
Discover learning styles and cultural frameworks

Discussions about differences don't always have to be heavy and difficult. Find playful ways to uncover the variety of ways people approach and understand things. One of my favorites is an activity I call "True Confessions in Four Corners." In a staff meeting, tell the group that you are going to ask a question and then designate each corner of the room with a possible answer to choose from. There is no right answer, and everyone gets to determine their own meaning for going to a particular corner. The debriefing after each round brings forth new insights and fondness among the staff.

When it comes to learning something new, I usually:

- read a book or a manual.

- seek out advice.

- look for a model.

- jump in and try it.

My family and culture taught me to view a person in authority as:

- someone to always be respected.

- someone to be suspicious of.

- someone to count on for help.

- someone to maneuver around.

When I'm upset with a family member or co-worker, the instinctive thing I want to do is:

- act like a dog.

- behave like an ostrich.

- fly like an eagle.

- move like a bear.

Principle:
Provide training choices for different needs and interests

If you look back again on something you learned in your adult life, consider what motivated you to pursue this. Most likely you had a compelling need or particular interest that led you to and sustained your learning. How can you translate this to your coaching of caregivers? Staff must feel a need for the knowledge or skill you are asking them to learn.

Hopefully, most of your coaching and mentoring is individualized. You may still have staff meetings focused on a training topic, but these should evolve out of staff input. Choosing a training focus for your program to pursue over time doesn't mean repeating the same training again and again. Rather, you can approach a topic with a variety of strategies and goals for different staff members. This models how you want them to create curriculum that is individualized for children.

Strategy:
Give staff opportunities to pursue their passions

Most directors are inclined to spend precious training dollars on identified weaknesses in staff. But if you heed the theories of adult learning and our principle of providing for different needs and interests, you will create opportunities for staff members to identify passions they want to pursue. They may need coaxing with activities of values clarification, telling stories, and sharing interests.

Ask teachers to each bring samples of something they are collecting: spoons, shells, buttons, pipes, postcards, antique tools, objects with a frog motif. Discuss what got them interested in this and any stories associated with the collection. On another occasion, have them bring a photograph or object that represents a triumph in their life. Spend time in a staff meeting having each person identify one thing they'd really like to understand or be able to do before they die. Find ways for your coaching to continue to stimulate this interest. It will enliven you and your staff and the experiences they offer to children.

Strategy:
Redefine appropriate topics for staff development

Because we have a workforce with limited training in early childhood education, we often have tunnel vision when it comes to thinking about staff development. Teachers typically need training on setting up learning environments, planning curriculum, child development, and a variety of health and safety concerns. But it's useful to broaden our notions about topics that are appropriate for staff development.

- Could you set up a series of workshops with an American Sign Language, Spanish, or Chinese instructor to help your staff work better with more diverse families?

- Consider scheduling training with a physical therapist on sensory integration activities, training with a mental health therapist on eating disorders, or time with an architect or landscaper focusing on principles of design.

- How might attending some cultural performances together enhance the development of your staff as a community?

Just as we want teachers to break out of the little boxes that confine their thinking about curriculum, you need to expand your definition of appropriate training.

Principle:
Emphasize dispositions as much as skills and knowledge

Teacher dispositions are as critical to their effectiveness as are skills and knowledge. I first began to think about the idea of teacher dispositions from reading the work of Lilian Katz. She defines a disposition as the habit of mind or tendency to respond to

situations in certain ways. Katz stresses that teacher educators should be trying to strengthen worthwhile dispositions in teachers and weaken those that are unhelpful.

Strategy:
Invent opportunities for discovery

With more expertise than a certain caregiver, it's often easy for directors to identify problems with what's happening. Sometimes you can walk into a room and immediately see something that needs fixing. As a coach focused on cultivating dispositions, resist the urge to immediately offer suggestions.

Invent strategies that will promote reflection and self-examination. For instance, rather than telling caregivers that their room arrangement is set up for continual conflicts between children, give them a way to discover this for themselves. I've used packages of colored sticky dots for this purpose, supplying teachers with dots to stick in the area of the room where they see conflict disrupting children's engaged play. At the end of the week, we discuss whether they've discovered any patterns in where conflicts tend to occur.

An activity like this may take a bit longer to solve a problem, but the results tend to be more substantial because effective dispositions are being cultivated.

Principle:
Build a community of listeners, observers, storytellers

Listening and observation skills are central to good teaching and collaboration with co-workers and parents. With each visit to a room, you have opportunities to coach caregivers and teachers by describing even a small conversation or activity you witness there. You can informally share detailed descriptions in quick conversations in the hallways and in staff meetings. This modeling shows staff that you value stories that come from children.

Strategy:
Cultivate observation skills with informal research projects

Rather than portraying staff development as a process where teachers learn from experts, encourage teachers to learn for themselves from careful observations. Identify a topic about children's behavior that seems to generate a lot of teacher attention. Consider a question related to this on which teachers could focus some observations. "What's the meaning of all this noise we're hearing in the block area?" "What skills do children use to get included in the play of others?" Provide some simple observation forms for them to document activities related to the question under investigation.

You may need to initially model and coach them in recognizing the details of children's conversation and play. Then collaborate in analyzing and hypothesizing about its meaning. Write up stories for newsletters or create documentation displays about your discoveries.

Informal research projects strengthen observation, documentation, and collaboration skills. Paying closer attention to the seemingly ordinary events of the classroom helps teachers see things in a new light. They are motivated to reflect on their previously unexamined responses to children. The stories of their discoveries can generate learning and excitement in others.

Principle:
Promote collaboration and mentoring relationships

You can both formally and informally encourage collaboration and peer coaching relationships across your program. This shouldn't be limited to old timers helping the newcomers, but rather a system of acknowledging that we all have things to learn from each other. If we want children to be sharing and helping each other, they need to see us doing this as well.

In a staff meeting, take time to identify the strengths of each staff member and of the program in each room. Probe to discover what might be called the signature feature, a particular attribute or skill that contributes something unique to your program. Begin an inquiry process as to who has what expertise.

Whether you develop a formal or informal peer mentoring system, this recognition will strengthen your learning community. Pairing people for collaborative tasks that cross rooms and age groups keeps the learning mutual and expanding.

Strategies for building collaborative or peer mentoring relationships:

- Choose a mutual focus for learning and set individual goals.

- Visit each other's rooms and rooms in other programs.

- Read and discuss relevant literature together.

- Tell stories of things you've observed related to your focus.

- Observe a child together and share notes.

- Examine children's portfolio collections together.

- Facilitate a staff meeting together.

- Write articles together for newsletters.

Principle:
Provide time and resources

It's obvious that for coaching to make a difference in teachers' lives, they need paid time away from children to think, talk, and plan. Providing this time in and of itself is a coaching strategy. It creates room for reflection, gathering thoughts, and collaborating with co-workers. Without adequate time and resources to do their jobs well, your staff will likely experience more frustration than refinement of their skills, more lethargy than learning from their teaching practice. Time for coaching and reflection is work time, not break time — which teachers also need.

Strategy:
Develop your budget with additional time for staff

Experiment with ways to reconfigure your current budget as you develop a strategic plan for generating more resources for staff development. What would happen if all the money allocated for training in your current budget was dispersed to teachers for extra time to meet, collaborate, and document? Perhaps they would learn just as much if not more than attending a workshop or conference. If they produced evidence in the form of documentation displays and improved teaching performance, wouldn't this seem justified? Set aside your urge to say "Yes, but…" and, with your staff, get your creative juices flowing. If you make it a priority, you can make it happen.

Margie Carter

Margie Carter is the co-founder of Harvest Resources Associates (www.ecetrainers.com) and the co-author of numerous books and early childhood videos. As she moves towards retirement years, her professional work is focused on highlighting and supporting the inspiring work of new leaders and uplifting the voices and leadership of teachers in the field.

Mentors as Teachers, Learners, and Leaders

by Marcy Whitebook and Dan Bellm

A New Wave of Mentoring Programs in the United States

Early childhood teachers face increasing standards and expectations about what they should know and be able to do in promoting children's early learning and development. This has led to a dramatic surge in the types and numbers of mentoring opportunities currently operating in the early care and education field. Mentoring is a relationship-based adult learning strategy intended to promote and support a teacher's awareness and refinement of her professional learning process and teaching practices. Historically, mentoring has been thought of as a strategy to support new teachers, often within the context of their pursuit of higher education, but mentoring now takes place in a wider range of settings, with variations in mentoring goals and mentor-protégé relationships. Most mentoring programs today are designed in the service of quality improvement and are supported by a blend of public and philanthropic dollars. Mentoring:

- can take place in a mentor's work setting, perhaps as a component of a protégé's participation in formal training or coursework.

- can take place in a protégé's work setting.

- may be voluntary.

- may be a required element of one's job or of a center's participation in a quality improvement initiative.

- may have fairly general and broad goals.

- may have narrowly defined or even prescriptive goals — for example, focused on preparing for an assessment or evaluation, improving a test score, or learning how to use a certain classroom tool or curriculum.

- can occur over a relatively short period of time, in relation to a specific goal.

- may be a year-long or multi-year process.

The structure of a mentoring program can have implications for how mentors are expected to do their work, who their protégés are, and why the protégés are participating. (See Chart 1 for a summary of the variations among mentoring programs.)

In order to reflect the changing mentoring terrain, and the multiple contexts in which mentoring now occurs, we felt that the time was right for a completely new version of an *Early Childhood Mentoring Curriculum* (first released in 1997, co-authored with Patty Hnatiuk). Our 2013 book, *Supporting Teachers as Learners: A Guide for Mentors and Coaches in Early Care and Education*, is intended for all who work as mentors or in other roles to educate and support teachers and family child care providers in their practice with children. As with early childhood teachers in general, mentors face increasing expectations about what they should know and be able to do in promoting early childhood practitioner's learning and development. Yet only about half the states have identified competencies for mentors and coaches, and many mentors are called upon to assume the complex task of supporting teachers as learners without appropriate preparation and support for their role.[1]

In this article we address three aspects of mentoring — mentors as teachers, mentors as learners, and mentors as leaders — that we believe are essential for developing a skilled corps of mentors who are charged with helping teachers of young children improve their practice.

Some Definitions and a Note on Terminology

While the terms 'mentoring' and 'coaching' are often used interchangeably, there can be significant distinctions between these two roles. Mentors tend to focus on the development of an individual teacher, and goals for the mentoring process are typically agreed upon mutually between the mentor and protégé — although mentoring relationships may differ, depending on the structure and intention of particular mentoring programs. In contrast, coaches may work either with individuals or with classroom teams as a group, and/or may have a set agenda for classroom improvement.

Often, however, the distinctions between mentoring and coaching become blurred in practice. In this article, as in our book, Supporting Teachers as Learners, we use the terms 'mentor' and 'mentoring' for the sake of consistency — but we provide concepts and activities that are relevant for mentors, coaches, and

others in technical assistance and support roles. We also use the term 'protégé' for the person with whom a mentor works; other terms that are sometimes used in the field are 'mentee', 'peer', or 'apprentice'. (See Chart 2 — Core Principles of Mentoring.)

Mentors as Teachers

Having a particular skill — even if we are highly proficient at it — doesn't necessarily mean that we can pass it on to someone else. Being a great baker or cook is probably a prerequisite for hosting a TV cooking show, but it certainly doesn't guarantee high ratings. The successful television chef doesn't just demonstrate her skills; she can describe what she's doing as she goes, taking us through the steps in an accessible way. The clarity and style of her actions and explanations are what draw us in as viewers.

So it is, too, with a good early childhood mentor. Mentors are 'articulate practitioners' who not only can demonstrate excellent skills with young children, families, and other adults in the early learning environment, but also talk about their skills and practices meaningfully with others. By bringing their own thinking and practice to light, mentors help protégés to become more articulate practitioners themselves.

To take one example: a mentor can demonstrate how she facilitates children's pre-math skills as they 'play store' in the dress-up corner — and she can explain the thinking behind her words and actions, as well as why she may have rejected other possible strategies. In doing so, she not only provides direct experience and information for her protégé, but she is modeling the cognitive and decision-making processes that underlie good teaching and its connection to how children learn. To be an effective teacher of adults, a mentor requires foundational knowledge about, and experience with, children and pedagogy. But the mentor toolkit also must include an ability to describe how and why she approaches teaching young children in particular ways, an understanding of how adults learn, and strategies to promote change.

Mentors as Learners

An effective mentor is committed to her own growth and development as a teacher of adults, and is willing to learn new skills and reflect upon her practice working with teachers of young children. A key part of her job is to periodically assess her own knowledge and skills in relation to working with protégés, and to identify her own ongoing learning goals. Because mentoring is both relationship-based and content-based, mentors need to consider their competence and needs for professional development in both arenas.

Mentoring should take place within an open and warm relationship, founded in mutual respect for what each person brings to the process, but it is more than this: it is a finely-tuned balance of support and challenge, focused on encouraging reflection, change, and growth. Most mentors will likely consider their skills very developed in some areas of relationship building, only somewhat developed in others, and perhaps not yet developed in others. For example, a mentor may feel she has a good grasp on principles of adult learning, and feel confident in assessing her protégé's teaching practices and identifying areas of strength and potential improvement. But she may feel less secure in navigating the dynamics of the mentor-protégé relationship and the context in which it occurs, particularly if the protégé's stated needs and goals do not align with her stage of teacher development and/or the goals of the mentoring program. Or a mentor may find herself working with a protégé whose ethnicity or culture is different from her own, leading her to recognize that she has not yet developed skills in asking and learning about her protégé's cultural traditions, and how they influence her approach to teaching.

Mentors are often expected to help their protégés strengthen various aspects of classroom management and children's learning, and no mentor is likely to consider herself an articulate practitioner in all of them. A mentor may assess her skills as well developed in promoting three- and four-year-old children's social and emotional development, but not in doing the same with infants and toddlers. Or she may consider herself effective in promoting children's literacy, but not their mathematical or scientific thinking. Even if she assesses herself as competent to 'do' something with children in one area, she may not feel she knows how to bring her own process to light for her protégé to consider.

A mentoring program, ideally, will actively help mentors develop strategies and access resources to address their ongoing development and effectiveness, by attending to various domains of the mentor's learning environment, including:

- **teaching supports** — whether the program structure assigns a manageable number of protégés to each mentor, and allows mentors sufficient opportunities to observe and meet with them.

- **learning community** — the program provides regular opportunities for learning and practicing mentoring skills and a designated person to help mentors identify specific learning objectives and strategies to achieve them.

- **job crafting** — whether mentors have the authority to select or adapt mentoring strategies based on the mentor's assessment of a protégé's learning needs.

- **adult well-being** — whether mentors receive appropriate compensation and benefits, and have fair and respectful working relationships.

- **program leadership** — whether mentors have regular access to a supervisor or coordinator who is knowledgeable about teaching both children and adults, familiar with their skills as mentors, and understands the challenges they face with protégés.

Mentors as Leaders

Mentors are uniquely situated at the intersection between where children are taught and cared for, where teachers and providers are educated and trained, and where early education policy is made. Mentors see the action close up, and thus their perspective on

Chart 1 — Variations in Mentoring Programs

There are a number of ways in which mentoring programs can differ:

Mentoring programs can vary in overall purpose to:
- provide collegial support through informal peer relationships.
- support the attainment of higher education (e.g. as a student teaching placement) and/or teacher certification.
- support protégés who are new to the field.
- improve retention of new and/or experienced teachers.
- help translate coursework theory into classroom practice.
- further a quality improvement initiative, such as a Quality Rating and Improvement System (QRIS) or the pursuit of program accreditation.
- help implement a curriculum or training model.

The program's desired outcomes may be to:
- achieve higher quality ratings or classroom assessment scores.
- improve specific instructional practices (such as those focused on early literacy).
- improve specific child outcomes (such as language development).

Mentors have varying work settings and job descriptions. They may:
- work within the same organization as protégés (for example, as a Head Start mentor-coach or within the same school district) or in a different organization.
- or may not be currently employed as classroom teachers.
- visit protégés' classrooms, or have protégés visit their classrooms.
- work with individual protégés or with classroom teams (the latter generally being a 'coaching' model).
- work with one protégé or with multiple protégés at a time.
- work with protégés who teach a variety of age groups of children within the birth-to-age-8 spectrum.
- work with protégés within a wide variety of time frames, from a matter of weeks or months to a year or more.
- be expected to include directors in various mentoring activities, or may have little involvement with directors.

Individual mentor-protégé goals and activities may be:
- collaboratively developed by the mentor and protégé, or prescribed by the mentoring initiative.
- wide-ranging in scope, or focused on particular content areas or skills.

Protégés may have varying reasons to participate in mentoring, such as:
- by choice, or as a required part of the job.
- a component (required or not) of a degree or training program.
- a mandate because of classroom quality ratings or other assessments.

Chart 2 — Core Principles of Mentoring

No matter where mentoring is taking place, however, we hold a core set of assumptions and principles about the mentoring process:

- The growth and development of children, and of adults, in early childhood settings are vitally linked.

- Like children, most adults learn best by having practical, job-related, hands-on opportunities to apply new ideas and information to real-life situations. The mentoring process provides a context for practicing and applying new skills, and for receiving guidance in teaching and caregiving practice.

- The first years of teaching are an especially important time for learning and growing, but effective mentoring can occur at any stage of an educator's career.

- Mentors should be directly experienced in the area(s) in which they are mentoring or coaching others.

- In order to be most effective, a mentor should be trained as one. While a mentor should have considerable experience and skill in early care and education, including child development and pedagogy, she should also receive training and support in the areas of adult learning and teacher development.

- Mentoring is not the same as supervision.

- A mentor is also a learner, and needs support, both as a teacher and as a learner.

From *Supporting Teachers as Learners: A Guide for Mentors and Coaches in Early Care and Education* by Marcy Whitebook and Dan Bellm, with Diana Schaack. Washington, DC: American Federation of Teachers, 2013.

---

how protégés are faring is a very important one. They are positioned, for example, to assess how realistic the mentoring program's objectives are, based on protégés' stages of teacher development, and how protégés' work environments impede or facilitate their efforts to improve their teaching.

There is, of course, no single ingredient that leads to effective teaching. While mentoring is essential, we know that it cannot entirely substitute for strong teacher education, or for good work environments that provide adequate teaching support, encourage teacher growth, and offer professional levels of compensation.

But mentors are in a unique position, at the nexus of policy and practice, to serve not only as agents of change who help protégés improve their teach-

ing practice and grow as professionals, but also as leaders and advocates who can contribute to broader improvements in adult work and learning environments in the field of early education. Mentors can help bring the voices of those who work daily with children into the discussion of how to improve services for all young children, since children's well-being is directly linked to the well-being of their teachers.

Resource

Supporting Teachers as Learners: A Guide for Mentors and Coaches in Early Care and Education, by Marcy Whitebook and Dan Bellm, with Diana Schaack, includes chapters on theories of adult learning and adult development; how to form and build strong relationships between mentors and protégés; skills and strategies for effective mentoring; and mentors as leaders who can help promote better adult work environments in the early education field. Available from Redleaf Press, www.redleafpress.org/Search.aspx?k=whitebook

End Notes

1 U.S. Department of Health and Human Services, Administration for Children and Families, & Head Start Bureau, (2005); NAEYC & NACCRRA, (2011); Zaslow, M., Tout, K., Halle, T., Whittaker, J., & Lavelle, B. (2010), *Toward the identification of features of effective professional development for early childhood educators: Literature review*. Washington, DC: Child Trends.

2 We credit this term to Ruby Takanishi, who used it in "The Unknown Teacher: Symbolic and Structural Issues in Teacher Education," her keynote address at the Midwest AEYC conference, Milwaukee, Wisconsin, 1980.

Marcy Whitebook and Dan Bellm

Marcy Whitebook and Dan Bellm began their careers in the 1970s as teachers of young children. Since that time, they have engaged in research, public education, policy development, training, and advocacy efforts focused on the early care and education workforce. Marcy directs the Center for the Study of Child Care Employment at the University of California, Berkeley.

Dan is an independent writer, editor, and Spanish-English translator.

The Spirit of Adult Play

by Bonnie Neugebauer

Roger sits on the sofa with Carrie and Martha, age 5, and asks: "Well, you girls must be about ready to get jobs! Have you found your own apartment yet?" Carrie and Martha eye him incredulously, then dissolve into giggles.

Delores joins Stephanie on the riding toy and together, adult and child, they whiz down the riding path, hair flying, smiles blazing.

Lynne and Keisha, age 25 or so, sit on the riverbank creating a miniature world with pinecones, rocks, and sticks. The focus of their bodies and their quiet, intense conversation exclude the rest of the campers.

Adults who play. They play with words and ideas. They use toys, invent props, appropriate resources for new purposes. They play with children and with other adults. They play because it is natural and because it makes them feel good. Children need these adults in their lives, people who will model the importance of play to living. But in so many early childhood programs, people have forgotten how to be playful. They are focused on order and routines, appearances and paperwork, agendas and lesson plans. There is no serendipity, no wonder, no surprise.

Some adults play naturally; they never forgot how. Other adults must relearn the joys of playfulness.

But play is consuming, and adults and children who would play must be willing to spend freely, to squander, to waste (if you will), to be extravagant with their:

Time — Play must exist in a context of timelessness. The process is valued beyond the outcome of the play, so it must be possible to continue the experience across blocks of time, even across days and weeks. The play must find its own end, just as it found its own beginning.

Energy — Play requires total commitment. Players need to focus their attention on what they are doing without regard for what is happening elsewhere.

There is no place for concern about the next activity or concurrent distractions. In play we are not afraid of what might prove difficult, or complex.

Resources — Play consumes resources. For a block city to grow, there must be enough blocks to meet the ever-expanding need. Castles require a beach-worth of sand. Paper sculptures require sufficient materials to rework ideas and fulfill projections.

Sense of Self — Play requires that one forget oneself. If self-conscious about their play, about how others will view either their play or the products of their play, children and adults are crippled. Their play is distorted by other consciousness.

Sense of Order — Play demands a certain amount of chaos. There must be room for using things and doing things in new ways. Play equipment and space must be flexible to meet the changing needs of the players. There must be storage for uncompleted play, and respect for unfinished spaces. Players require a degree of uncertainty and support for taking risks. Play is nurtured when there is no labeling of wrong and right.

Joy — Play without enjoyment is just plain hard work. Players need to laugh, and boast, and practice. There are many choices to be made, and each is a challenge. Play brings out the best in each of us.

It is often said that play is the work of children. What then, is the play of adults? For a fortunate few, work is play. But for far greater numbers of adults, work is work; and there is not enough time for real, natural play. Or we are not sure enough of ourselves to take risks and to be spontaneous. What would happen if we approached everything in our lives with a more playful spirit? How would this playful spirit change our workday, our parenting, our lovemaking? With effort, the play of adults can be life.

Towards a More Playful Spirit

What would happen if…

parents found me playing when they arrived at the center? What would I be doing?

parents came to the center to play with their children? How can I make this happen?

teachers were comfortable playing during the workday? Would it be okay to play alone or with other adults, or would it only be okay to play with children?

I turned my most hateful task into play? How could I accomplish this?

I didn't worry about making mistakes or failing? What if I didn't care about making a fool of myself?

I did the things that I really enjoy frequently? What are those things in my life?

Bonnie Neugebauer

Bonnie Neugebauer is editor of *Exchange Magazine* and co-founder of the World Forum Foundation.

the Art of LEADERSHIP

DEVELOPING PEOPLE
IN EARLY CHILDHOOD ORGANIZATIONS

3 CHAPTER 3
Appraising Staff

Performance Appraisals: One Step in a Comprehensive
Staff Supervision Model *by Susan Kilbourne*. 78

Monitoring, Measuring, and Evaluating Staff Performance *by Kay M. Albrecht* 83

Guidelines for Effective Use of Feedback *by Roger Neugebauer* 87

Looking Inside: Helping Teachers Assess Their Beliefs and Values *by Paula Jorde Bloom* 91

Evaluating Staff Performance: A Valuable Training Tool *by Margie Carter* 94

Overcome the Fear of Firing *by Roger Neugebauer* 97

Performance Appraisals:

One Step in a Comprehensive Staff Supervision Model

by Susan Kilbourne

Performance reviews, while stressful, can prepare your employees for the next stages of their career. The best performance reviews are those where the supervisor knows the employee's skills and talents and offers suggestions on how to use those talents to develop other areas of job performance and professional growth.

Open, honest, and frequent communication between teachers and supervisors is essential to developing and maintaining a strong faculty team. Positive feedback is a necessary ingredient in building effective performance. One way that supervisors can establish mutual understanding of job expectations is by reviewing job descriptions with new employees. Effective orientation that ensures a clear understanding of expectations for performance is also important at the beginning of a good relationship between employee and employer. Once an employee understands what is expected, it is easier to deliver consistent results with mutually beneficial outcomes for both the employee and the organization.

use the interview process to guide expectations for the position. Both the employee and the organization are set up for success when clear expectations and job responsibilities are outlined from the beginning. Employees need to know the expectations of the job as well as the specific expectations the supervisor has for each employee and their respective positions.

It helps if training needs are established early on so that the supervisor can suggest training opportunities to meet the professional development goals of the new employee. Questions relating to the candidate's philosophy of learning, discipline, and family relationships can help the interviewer determine if a candidate is a good philosophical match for the position. Additional questions regarding work ethic and professional development may indicate if the candidate is self-motivated and willing to learn new skills and teaching practices. Potential candidates may bring documentation of training certificates, degrees earned, or a portfolio of work to demonstrate their desire for continued learning.

The Interview

Laying the foundation for good performance review is not easy. It takes preparation from the time an employee interviews for the position. Some managers

Orientation

Orientation is critical to the success of a new employee. During the orientation phase, an employee can develop meaningful connections with others within the organization. These connections are critical in helping the new person feel welcome and an important member of the team. Additionally, there is no better time to acquaint the new employee with the culture of the organization and to become familiar with the manner in which the center conducts day-to-day operations. Orientation may include introductions to other faculty members, the establishment of a mentor relationship, tours and observations of daily operations, as well as formal training on the practices and procedures that will ensure their success. Orientation should introduce the employee to job expectations and give them a sense of the culture of the center. Parents and other staff members play a key role in introducing the new employee to the culture and helping them feel welcome. A sample orientation checklist is provided.

Ongoing Performance Reviews

Regular observation and feedback sessions with employees help them to develop desirable job skills more quickly and to know what is expected of them. After the initial hire, orientation, and the probationary period (typically 90 days), it is important for supervisors to check in with new employees and conduct a quick review. This review, around the third month of employment, offers an opportunity to discuss training needs and set goals for the next performance period. This is an excellent time for the supervisor to provide specific feedback and guide the employee to success within the organization. Many organizations require a 90-day review. At this time, the employee and supervisor meet and discuss progress on the original orientation plan and basics of the job description. Strengths, development areas, and goals may be included. Employees who reflect on their teaching practices and jointly set goals for continued improvement are more likely to develop better teaching strategies. Information from formal classroom observation and feedback sessions may be included in the review. The following are some sample questions to consider for a 90-day review:

■ What is going well in the classroom?

■ What questions do you have about your job?

■ What goals do you have for your room?

■ How can I help support you in achieving those goals?

The purpose of performance appraisals is three-fold. First, they give employees the opportunity to discuss their performance with their supervisor, comparing it to the organizational standards set by the supervisor and the organization. Second, performance appraisals give the supervisor a means to discuss and identify the strengths and challenges for each employee. The format of the performance appraisal allows the supervisor an opportunity to recommend a specific program of training to help the employee improve performance. Finally, the performance review provides the supervisor with a basis for salary recommendations. By evaluating each employee's contributions to the organization, a supervisor can evaluate relative contributions of each employee and suggest salary increases consistent with the goals and achievements of each individual with respect to organizational standards.

Annual Performance Appraisals

Fairness and objectivity are critical in measuring job performance. In an effort to be as objective as possible, supervisors may wish to establish standardized performance criteria. In the field of early childhood education, many tools are available for your use. Recently, when conducting training for managers, one experienced manager, Melanie Brooks from the GlaxoSmithKline Child Development Center, told me she always asks employees to bring samples of their work to the performance review conference. These samples might include sample lesson plans, children's journals, sample daily notes, and examples of documentation panels the teacher has created. This type of documentation clearly demonstrates how the employee is meeting job expectations.

These samples can serve as the basis of a professional portfolio that the supervisor and employee can create together to document the employee's personal and professional growth. Additional methods for gathering objective information are:

■ parent surveys.

■ parent letters.

■ awards nominations.

■ licensing files.

■ peer reviews.

■ health department reports.

■ student portfolios.

■ student assessments.

■ sample daily notes or classroom newsletters.

■ evaluative tools such as the *Infant-Toddler* or *Preschool Environmental Rating Scales* (ITERS or ECERS) and the National Association for the Education of Young Children's (NAEYC) classroom observation booklet.

■ other internal evaluative tools can prove helpful as well.

Another method of conducting a performance evaluation is a '360 review,' which can provide an accurate evaluation with input from all constituents with whom a person interfaces in her job. The prospect of having so many people evaluate one's performance can be daunting. Such a review solicits feedback from peers, parents, supervisors, and perhaps a client or parent board. Input from a variety of perspectives provides insight that only multiple people can offer. The result is a more accurate and comprehensive review with input from many perspectives. Goals for improving the curriculum, customer service, and teamwork are more easily established and it is easier to measure progress in this model. A comprehensive review is more difficult to achieve with the limited perspective of only one or two people.

Intended to help employees achieve professional goals and improve teaching practices, performance reviews are most effective when they are comprehensive and draw from many different sources of information. The employee may choose five or six people with whom they work closely and ask them to offer feedback in the areas where they are familiar with the person's performance. The supervisor uses the feedback when working jointly with the employee to set goals for the next performance period. A trusting environment is needed to support the effective implementation of this type of review and may be better suited for more tenured employees.

Retention

According to training materials by Media Partners entitled *Keeping the Good Ones* (Media Partners, 2001), the top three reasons employees leave are because they do not feel connected to their boss, they do not feel appreciated, and they do not feel they are growing professionally. When a supervisor takes the time to connect with an employee and to help them make other connections in the organization, the supervisor is taking the first step to retaining that employee.

After a solid orientation and a few months on the job, it is time for the supervisor to meet with the employee to assess job performance and determine future training needs. During this meeting, the supervisor and employee should have the opportunity to outline progress and future goals. This meeting helps the employee understand job expectations and have some measure of control over future training opportunities. This meeting should communicate to the employee that his work is appreciated and that opportunities for professional growth are available within the organization. During this meeting, goals should be established to support training and growth for the employee. Goal reviews should occur regularly and continual revisions should occur based on the individual and on changing organizational needs.

Retention is increased when staff is appreciated for outstanding work performance and when the feedback is based on pre-determined goals. Appreciation for a good day's work comes in many forms.

However, it is critical that the supervisor make an effort to recognize good work in a way that is meaningful to the employee. A simple "thank you" can go a long way in helping a person feel that their contribution matters. When a "thank you" is in the form of a written note, it is even more powerful.

Conclusion

Quality employees are gently molded and sculpted. I believe people want to do good work and have a basic need to achieve goals they help establish. By helping individuals set and meet goals, a supervisor can help others accomplish great work and enjoy the benefits of feeling a job has been well done. When an employee fails, a supervisor has the opportunity to look at what could have been done to enhance the chances of success for that employee and what, if anything, the supervisor could have done to increase their chance of success. Behind most great teachers is a solid director or manager leading the charge for good performance by setting expectations during the interview process, thoroughly orienting new employees, offering regular observation and feedback, and helping the employee set and meet professional and personal goals.

References

Compact Disc. (2001). *Keeping the good ones*. Media Partners, 911 Western Avenue, Seattle, WA 98104.

National Association for the Education of Young Children. (2006). *Code of ethical conduct*. Washington, DC: Author.

For further reading

Armstrong, S., & Appelbaum, M. (2003). *Stress-free performance appraisals: Turn your most painful management duties into a powerful motivational tool*. Franklin Lakes, NJ: Career Press.

Susan Kilbourne

Susan Kilbourne is a Regional Manager for Bright Horizons Family Solutions with oversight of centers serving SAS Institute, Inc. in Cary, North Carolina; Bright Horizons at Tyson's Greensboro Drive in McLean, Virginia; Bright Horizons at East End in Washington, DC; and a back-up center for the WilmerHale Law Firm in Washington, DC. Additionally, she has supported child care operations for the International Monetary Fund, George Washington University, Booz Allen Hamilton Family Center, and School's Out services for Verizon Wireless in Virginia and West Virginia. She has been in the early care and education field for 22 years working as a teacher, assistant director, director, executive director, area manager, and regional manager. Prior to entering the early education field, Susan worked in the public schools in Rome, New York, with Junior and Senior High students for two years.

New Employee Orientation Checklist				
Topic	**Covered By**	**Initials**	**Date**	**Employee Initials**
Tour center				
Schedule				
Assign mentor				
Complete paperwork				
Employee handbook				
Family handbook				
Licensing standards				
NAEYC standards				
NAEYC *Code of Ethical Conduct*				
Benefits overview				
Job description				
Positive guidance				
Mandated reporting				
Bottle feeding procedures				
Diaper changing procedures				
Hand washing procedures				
Food service procedures				
Curriculum resources				
Emergency preparedness procedures				
Communication protocol				
Classroom opening procedures				
Classroom closing procedures				
Center goals				
Date orientation completed:				
Employee signature:				

Monitoring, Measuring, and Evaluating Staff Performance

by Kay M. Albrecht

Although every director would agree that teachers need to be regularly evaluated, many find little time to do it. Nevertheless, there are a number of good reasons to monitor, measure, and evaluate teacher performance:

- To identify good teachers so they can be recognized and rewarded for their excellence.

- To identify poor teachers so they can be counseled into a more appropriate career choice.

- To identify teaching skill deficits so they can be improved through training.

The critical first step is to establish your program philosophy. It is impossible to determine evaluation criteria until you are in touch with the philosophical principles, which guide your program. Include your staff in the process of establishing your philosophy, particularly if you do not have a written philosophy to guide you. The philosophy statement that emerges as staff members consider their beliefs about children, families, and programs will guide you in all of your efforts. Not only will it guide your behavior, it will also clearly articulate to parents what they can expect from your program. Because parents know what to expect from your program, they are more likely to be satisfied.

The next step is to identify the teaching behaviors that support your philosophy, as well as those that are in conflict with it. For example, if you believe that children need security and nurturance in the care and early education setting, you will value teachers who respond to children needing affection and security by comforting, stroking, and soothing them. Teachers who use these skills are demonstrating philosophically compatible teaching behaviors. Teachers who respond with comments like "big boys (girls) don't cry when they fall down" are showing insensitivity to children's needs and are demonstrating philosophically incompatible teaching skills.

When developing your competency list, include categories of behaviors such as professional skills (reading professional publications), personal skills (punctuality), interactive skills (bending or stooping to the child's eye level, calling children by their names), parent relations skills (communicating to parents necessary information about the child's day), and peer relations skills (avoiding nonproductive conversation with co-teachers while on duty).

As you go about describing the behaviors, which you want teachers to demonstrate, avoid the inclusion of behaviors you cannot see, like *'seems to understand children.'* Instead, choose behaviors that can be easily observed in the natural setting of the classroom. *'Sees that children are dressed appropriately for existing temperatures throughout the day'* is a competency that can be readily observed on the playground or perhaps at nap time. It is also important to limit the number of skills you identify to a reasonable number. While you want your observations to provide you with a measure of teacher performance, you do not want it to be cumbersome and unmanageable.

Finally, put the skills identified into a usable format. A checklist is often the easiest. Listing the skills down one side of a page allows you to take anecdotal notes about the skills and behaviors on the other side of the page. Having a usable format will facilitate the gathering of supportive data through observation. Be sure that your format allows you to easily identify which skills you have not seen demonstrated and need to observe for or plan to address through training.

Monitoring Classroom Behavior

Monitoring the classroom behavior of teachers is the most difficult part of the process because it is usually perceived by directors as time consuming. The following suggestions may help:

- **Set up a schedule for monitoring skills.** Observe in the natural setting of the classroom where teachers are regularly assigned.

- **Share with teachers the intent of your observations, what you are observing, and the schedule of your observations.** If teachers know in advance that you are observing for particular philosophically supportive teaching behaviors and that you plan to observe them more than just once, they will be more likely to see the process as positive and less likely to be intimidated by your observations.

- **Vary the time of the day during which you observe.** If you observe only at transition times, you are likely to miss certain key skills. On the other hand, observing the way a teacher handles transitions is an important piece of information to have. One or two observations in the morning, one or two at transition times, one observation during outdoor play, and one observation in the late afternoon would be a good basis for beginning the feedback dialogue.

- **Vary the length of your observations.** During interest or learning center time, there may be opportunities to observe many teaching skills. In this case, a 10- to 15-minute observation may be required. Observing the storytelling skills of a teacher may require only three or four minutes of observation.

- **Observe all the time.** This is the most important thing to remember. As directors manage by walking around, they see a great deal of teaching behavior taking place. When you go into a classroom to get the lunch count, look around to see what skills the teacher might be demonstrating. By capitalizing on observation moments like these, you will easily gather documentation of skills without extensive time dedicated to the process.

- **Resist the tendency to reach a conclusion after one or two observations.** You are looking to see which of the identified teaching skills is a part of the teacher's behavior over a period of time. Teachers may handle situations differently depending on a variety of variables. Observing more than once will allow you to differentiate those behaviors that are a part of a teacher's repertoire and those that are emerging or not present.

- **Record what you see.** Take notes during your observation in an anecdotal or running diary format. In order for the information you gather from your observations to be useful, it must be based on what you see rather than the way you feel about what you see. For example:

Miss Jan looked up from her story to see Jon and his mother at the door. She stopped her story and said, "Excuse me, children, I'll be right back. Jon is here and I need to say hello to his mother." She walked over to the door, stooped down to Jon's level and said in a pleasant voice, "Good morning, Jon." Then she looked up at his mother and said in a pleasant voice, "I hope you enjoyed the holidays. Jon was looking forward to Christmas at his grandparents. I hope he'll tell us about it later." Looking back at Jon, Miss Jan said, "You can join me in the library center for a story if you like. Say goodbye to Mommy and I'll help you put your things in your cubby." Miss Jan and Jon walked toward his cubby as he waved goodbye to his mother.

This anecdotal report gives a number of clues to this teacher's skills. We know that she stoops to the child's eye level to interact, greets both parents and children upon arrival at the classroom, gathers information from the parent to use in individualizing her interactions, is aware of the activities of the entire group even when dealing with part of it, and so on. The brief interchange may have taken only two or three minutes and may have been observed as the director was returning from escorting a new family to an adjoining classroom. By focusing on the gathering of anecdotal information, it is possible to avoid the biggest roadblock to the system — making judgments based on inaccurate and/or incomplete information.

Providing Feedback to Teachers

Now that you have gathered documentation of the teaching skills, provide feedback to each staff member. To be effective, feedback must be regular and directed. It is often possible to provide feedback to teachers informally. A brief comment at naptime about the sensitive handling of a classroom conflict provides the teacher with immediate information about how you view her skills. Sharing how you handled a similar situation may provide a teacher with some new ideas about how to handle the situation if it arises again. It may also be possible to make a brief positive comment about what you observed when teachers were not involved directly with children. As valuable as informal feedback is, it cannot substitute for formal feedback in a constructive setting. New teachers need feedback early in their teaching experiences, as often as once a month. More experienced teachers need formal, structured feedback at least two or three times a year.

During the feedback session, the director should share with the teacher the information she gathered during her observations. The exchange of information is most helpful if it is specific. A brief recount of the skills you observed when Jon and his mother arrived at the center would be a good way to begin.

Share the competency strengths you observed first. Talk about the skills that are in place. Give several examples from your notes. Be sure to include the subtle messages received from tone of voice, facial expressions, and body language.

Identify the one or two skills that you did not see demonstrated or that were inappropriately demonstrated. This discussion will be the real guts of the feedback conference. It should provide the teacher with information about how you perceive her behavior, as well as how you would like to see it changed. Both pieces of information are crucial. Giving feedback is not enough. It must be accompanied with specific guidance on how to change the behavior in question.

Following Up with Training

Sometimes the appropriate guidance cannot be given in the feedback conference alone. If this is the case, a training plan must be developed. The purpose of a training plan is to identify how the teacher will go about modifying her behavior or learn new teaching skills. The basis of the training plan is the director's evaluation of the teacher's weak skills. It should include the specific skills to be developed and improved, the training methods to be used, and the responsible person.

Because you have observed the skills of all of your staff members, you may be able to identify a teacher who has excellent skills in an area another teacher needs to improve. If this kind of situation can be developed, both teachers may benefit. One may benefit from the opportunity to improve her teaching skill; the other may benefit from the personal satisfaction of being recognized for having superior skills.

Directors may also be in the position to provide the needed training themselves. Because they have invested time in carefully monitoring, accurately measuring, and thoroughly evaluating each teacher's performance, training can be specific, timely, and efficiently accomplished. Also, training is better received because it is not a repetition of information skilled teachers already have. As a result, directors can be confident that their limited training time is well spent and effective.

As difficult as it is, we all must recognize that some staff members may not have the motivation or ability to develop their teaching skills to the desired level. In these cases, the director must face the difficult task of terminating a staff member. Supported by the specific knowledge collected in the monitoring, measuring, and evaluation process, the director can be certain that she has made the proper decision and has treated the staff member fairly. Without the documentation, directors may tend to avoid confronting inappropriate behavior to the detriment of young children.

It is human nature to want approval from our supervisors and peers. It is the director's job to be certain that messages of approval relate to real behavior and not to the absence of feedback. Setting up systems to carefully monitor, accurately measure, and thoroughly evaluate teacher competence will assure that teachers get the kind of approval that increases their motivation, job satisfaction and commitment, and positions them to grow and develop as individuals and teachers.

Kay M. Albrecht

Kay Albrecht, Ph.D., Houston, Texas, shared coaching responsibilities in First Relationships, wrote *Social Emotional Tools for Life: An Early Childhood Teacher's Guide* with Michelle Forrester, authored *The Right Fit: Recruiting, Selecting, and Orienting Staff*, now in a second edition, and created Out of the Box Early Childhood Training Kits for Exchange Press.

Guidelines for Effective Use of Feedback

by Roger Neugebauer

One of the most critical challenges facing an early childhood director is improving staff performance. A variety of tools are available to help a director meet this challenge: in-house training, annual appraisals, workshops, conferences, college classes, and training films. One of the least glamorous of these tools, providing feedback, is, in fact, the most effective.

With proper feedback, teachers can better control and improve their own performance; without proper feedback, teachers operate blindly, not knowing when their efforts succeed or fail. According to George F. J. Lehner, "... feedback helps to make us more aware of what we do and how we do it, thus increasing our ability to modify and change our behavior ... " (Lehner).

Just how blindly teachers operate without feedback was demonstrated in a study at the University of Michigan (McFadden). Twenty preschool teachers were interviewed about their teaching philosophies and methods. They all expressed a preference for teaching based on the discovery model. They expressed attitudes favoring a non-authoritarian, non-directive approach by the teacher. They preferred to show verbal concern and approval rather than disapproval. This was how they described their teaching.

Yet when they were actually observed in the classroom, their behavior was quite different. Observers found their classrooms to be predominantly teacher controlled and teacher centered. Their statements to children characterizing support, approval, or encouragement were fewer than 10% of their total statements (Schwertfeger). Without feedback, teachers may well be operating with false assumptions about the nature of their behavior and its effect on children and parents.

But as anyone who has tried to give advice to a teacher about her teaching style well knows, being effective at giving feedback is not an easy task. The natural tendency is for teachers to become defensive when feedback about their performance is presented. This reaction occurs when the receiver perceives a threat to her position in the organization, to her standing in the group, or to her own self-image.

When individuals become defensive, they are unlikely to accept, or even hear, feedback that is being offered. Instead of focusing on the message, a person reacting defensively "... thinks about how he appears to others; how he may be seen more favorably; how he may win, dominate, impress, or escape punishment; and/or how he may avoid or mitigate a perceived or an anticipated attack" (Gibb).

Defensiveness is increased when the receiver perceives feedback to be critical. As Douglas McGregor observes, "The superior usually finds that the effectiveness of the communication is inversely related to the subordinates' need to hear it. The more serious the criticism, the less likely is the subordinate to accept it" (McGregor).

Since teachers need feedback to improve their performance, it is important that a director become skilled at giving feedback that is helpful in a way that does not arouse their defensiveness. The following are recommendations on giving effective feedback:

■ **Feedback should focus on behavior, not the person.** In giving feedback, it is important to focus on what a person does rather than on what the person is. For example, you should say to a teacher "You talked considerably during the staff meeting" rather than "You're a loudmouth." According to George F. J. Lehner, "When we talk in terms of 'personality traits' it implies inherited constant qualities difficult, if not impossible, to change. Focusing on behavior implies that it is something related to a specific situation that might be changed" (Lehner). It is less threatening to a teacher to hear comments about her behavior than about her traits.

■ **Feedback should focus on observations, not inferences.** Observations are what we can see or hear in the behavior of another person. Inferences are interpretations we make based on what we hear or see (Lehner). Inferences are influenced by the observer's frame of references and attitudes. As such, they are much less likely to be accurate and to be acceptable to the person observed.

Inferences are much more likely to cause defensiveness.

■ **Feedback should focus on descriptions, not judgments.** In describing an event, a director reports an event to a teacher exactly as it occurred. A judgment of this event, however, refers to an evaluation in terms of good or bad, right or wrong, nice or not nice. Feedback, which appears evaluative, increases defensiveness (Gibb). It can readily be seen how teachers react defensively to judgments that are negative or critical. But it is often believed that positive judgments — praise — can be very effective as a motivational and learning tool. However, studies have shown that the use of praise has little long-term impact on employees' performance (Baehler). Often praise arouses defensiveness rather than dispelling it. Parents, teachers, and supervisors so often 'sugarcoat' criticism with praise ("You had a great lesson today, but ...") that "when we are praised, we automatically get ready for the shock, for the reproof" (Farson).

■ **Feedback should be given unfiltered.** There is a tendency for a director to sort through all the observations she makes of a teacher, and all the comments she receives about a teacher, and to pass along that information that she, the director, judges to be important or helpful. This filtering of feedback may diminish its value to the teacher. According to Peter F. Drucker, "People can control and correct performance if given the information, even if neither they nor the supplier of information truly understand what has to be done or how" (Drucker).

■ **Feedback should be given in small doses.** George F. J. Lehner has observed that "to overload a person with feedback is to reduce the possibility that he may use what he receives effectively" (Lehner). Accumulating observations and comments to share with a teacher in periodic large doses may be efficient for the director in terms of time management, but it may make the feedback too voluminous for the teacher to deal with effectively.

■ **Feedback should be given on a timely basis.**
If a teacher is given feedback about an incident in her classroom on the day that it occurs, she is much more likely to benefit from this feedback than if it is given to her days or weeks later. When feedback is given close to an event, the recipient is likely to remember all aspects of the event clearly, and thus is able to fit the feedback into a complete picture. When feedback is far removed from the event, the event will be less well remembered and the feedback will make less sense.

An extreme, but not atypical, example of untimely feedback is the annual appraisal. An annual appraisal is an effort to give feedback about performance over the past 365 days. Not only does this concentrated dose of feedback cause information overload, it also is offered at a time removed from the behavior itself. As such, it "is not a particularly effective stimulus to learning" (McGregor). Studies have shown that to be effective, performance appraisals "should be conducted not annually, but on a day-to-day basis" (Levinson).

■ **Feedback should be given to the teacher as his tool to control his own performance.**
A teacher is much more likely to benefit from feedback if it is given without strings attached, to use as he sees fit. If a director provides feedback ("The children were restless during circle time today") and then offers advice on how to use it ("I think you should have it earlier in the day"), the teacher is very likely to react defensively over this effort to control his behavior. "The real strength of feedback," according to Drucker, "is clearly that the information is the tool of the worker for measuring and directing himself."

■ **Avoid giving mixed messages.** Through their bodies, eyes, faces, postures, and senses people can communicate a variety of positive or negative attitudes, feelings, and opinions. While providing verbal feedback to a teacher, a director can communicate a conflicting message with her body language. For example, when verbally communicating a nonjudgmental description of

a playground scene, a director may be telecasting very disapproving signals to the teacher with the tension in her voice or the expression on her face. When presented with such mixed messages, a teacher invariably elects to accept the nonverbal message as the director's true meaning. As a result feedback gets distorted, and an atmosphere of distrust is created. "Right or wrong, the employee feels that you are purposely hiding something or that you are being less than candid" (Hunsaker).

To avoid communicating mixed messages, you should not give feedback when you are angry, upset, or excited. Wait until you cool down, so that you can keep your emotions under control as you talk. Also, you should develop the habit of monitoring your voice tone, facial expressions, and body language whenever you give feedback. Being aware of your body language can help you keep it consistent with your verbal language (Needell).

■ **Check for reactions.** Just as you give messages with your body language as you give feedback, the recipient signals her reaction to it with her body language. You should tune in to these signals as you talk. As Phillip Hunsaker recommends, "Constantly be on the lookout for nonverbal signals that indicate that your line of approach is causing your employees to become uncomfortable and lose interest. When this happens, change your approach and your message accordingly" (Hunsaker).

■ **Be open to feedback, yourself.** To develop an effective working relationship, you need feedback from your employees on their reactions to your behavior as much as they need feedback from you. According to organizational psychologist Harry Levinson, "In a superior-subordinate relationship, both parties influence each other, and both have a responsibility for the task." In order to accomplish this task, they must be able to talk freely to each other, and each must have the sense of modifying the other. "Specifically, the subordinate must be permitted to express his feelings about what the superior is doing in the relationship and what the subordinate would like him to do to further the accomplishment of the task" (Levinson).

■ **Encourage a team approach to feedback.** As director, you have a myriad of important tasks in addition to upgrading staff performance. Therefore, it is not possible for you to free up enough time to provide staff members all the feedback they need to improve their performance. In order to provide an ongoing flow of feedback information, you need to enlist all staff members to be feedback givers to each other. First, you must create an atmosphere in your center that encourages staff members to accept responsibility for helping each other improve. Second, you need to train staff members on the proper ways to give feedback. Feedback given in a judgmental, personal, or untimely fashion can be devastating and can poison interpersonal relations. Training can take the form of reviewing the guidelines discussed above in a staff meeting, by doing some role-playing, and by having staff members give each other feedback on how they give feedback. Most of all, staff members can learn to be effective feedback givers if you serve as a good model in the way you give feedback.

McGregor, D. (1960). *The human side of enterprise.* New York: McGraw-Hill Book Company.

Needell, C. K. (1963, January). "Learning to Level with Employees." *Supervisory Management.*

Schwertfeger, J. (1972). "Issues in Cooperative Training" in D. N. McFadden (editor), *Planning for action.* Washington, DC: NAEYC.

Roger Neugebauer

Roger Neugebauer is publisher of *Exchange Magazine* and a co-founder of the World Forum Foundation.

References

Baehler, J. R. (1980). *The new manager's guide to success.* New York: Praeger Publishers.

Drucker, P. F. (1974). *Management: Tasks, responsibilities, practices.* New York: Harper and Row Publishers.

Farson, R. E. (1963, September/October). "Praise Reappraised." *Harvard Business Review.*

Gibb, J. R. (1971). "Defensive Communication." In *Organizational psychology,* D. A. Kolb (editor). Englewood Cliffs, NJ: Prentice-Hall Inc.

Hunsaker, P. L., & Alessandra, A. J. (1980). *The art of managing people.* Englewood Cliffs, NJ: Prentice-Hall Inc.

Lehner, G. F. J. (1978, June). "Aids for Giving and Receiving Feedback." *Exchange.*

Levinson, H. (1981). *The exceptional executive.* Cambridge: Harvard University Press.

Looking Inside: Helping Teachers Assess Their Beliefs and Values

by Paula Jorde Bloom

Directors often lament how difficult it is to change teachers so that teaching practices are more developmentally appropriate and interactions with parents and other staff are more professional. The reason for the difficulty is that change efforts typically focus on increasing teachers' knowledge base. Clearly, knowledge is important; the workshops, the college classes, the books and articles are essential to expanding teachers' repertoire of instructional strategies. But knowledge is only part of the equation when it comes to helping teachers grow in professional competence. Directors must also help teachers become reflective practitioners. And reflection begins with an examination of one's own belief system.

Teachers' attitudes and beliefs about children provide the foundation for their philosophy of teaching. Because beliefs are grounded in one's values, they have a strong impact on shaping behavior. Teachers' values also govern how they will react when confronted with the inevitable ethical dilemmas that occur from time to time.

The assessment tool at the end of this article was designed to help teachers reflect on their attitudes and beliefs about children, parents, and their role in the classroom. The information gleaned from this self-assessment will help directors better understand the undergirding values and beliefs that drive the teaching practices they observe. Without clarification of these values, it is difficult to help teachers set goals for changing attitudes and behaviors.

This assessment can be used in a variety of ways. In the interviewing and hiring process, it can be used to help understand the belief system of prospective teachers. This information is essential if directors want to ensure that the beliefs and values of new staff are consonant with the shared beliefs and stated philosophy of the center.

The assessment can also be used as a springboard for discussion at a staff meeting. The director can distribute the assessment to teachers a few days before the meeting. Teachers can complete it at work or take it home where they may have fewer distractions. In either case, it is important to tell teachers that there are no right or wrong answers.

The completed assessments can be collected prior to the meeting and the responses to each of the eight questions in Part I noted on a large piece of news-print. It is not necessary to indicate which teacher made which comment. The eight sheets of newsprint can then be displayed on the walls in the room where the staff meeting will be held. The results of Part II can be summarized by simply noting the number of times a trait or characteristic was noted by teachers as being an important outcome of children's experience in the program.

If an open, nonjudgmental atmosphere exists during the staff meeting, a lively discussion should ensue about how each of the responses relates to the written philosophy and educational objectives of the center. A word of caution, though. When we discuss beliefs, we tap into teachers' core value systems. Tact and sensitivity to differing points of view is essential.

It is critical in such discussions that the director, as facilitator, avoid any hint of moralizing, criticizing, or judging the comments made by teachers. If teachers feel threatened, they will either shut down and refuse to share their inner feelings about these important issues or they will get defensive and assume a confrontational posture. Both are counterproductive to the goal of the group exercise.

Through an active, reflective listening process, the director can assist teachers in identifying and articulating the beliefs and values that undergird their teaching philosophy. The goal is to help teachers reflect on the source of their beliefs and begin to discuss how important parents, religion, early school experiences, and educational training are in shaping one's values. When conducted in a nonthreatening way, such group discussions can help teachers gain greater insight into how their beliefs guide what they do in the classroom every day.

Subsequent staff meetings might tackle thornier issues related to teachers' values and beliefs about the curriculum, instruction, and the teacher's role in promoting children's learning. For example, teachers can be asked to share their beliefs regarding the extent to which they believe child care experiences impact children's overall development and learning.

Recent research in this area has found that many early childhood teachers in this country embrace the belief that children's learning is largely determined by influences outside the center, in the genes and social background of the children. This belief is in sharp contrast to teacher beliefs in countries like Japan, where teachers at all levels of the educational system believe that achievement is a product more of effort than inherent talent. Teachers in Japan tend to believe their efforts in promoting student learning can make a difference.

Below are several statements that can serve as discussion starters about different values and beliefs that undergird educational practice. Teachers can brainstorm to generate additional statements to add to this list:

- Practice makes perfect.

- Telling is teaching.

- Parents don't value teachers' knowledge and expertise.

- Boys are naturally better at math than girls.

- Competition is necessary to motivate learning.

- The teacher is an authority that should not be questioned.

- Responding too quickly to crying children will spoil them.

Paula Jorde Bloom

Paula Jorde Bloom is associate professor of early childhood education at National-Louis University in Evanston, Illinois. Dr. Bloom is the author of several books, including *Avoiding Burnout* (New Horizons), *A Great Place to Work* (NAEYC), and *Living and Learning with Children* (New Horizons).

Values Clarification

Values are enduring beliefs — ideas that we cherish and regard highly. Values influence the decisions we make and the course of action we follow. Some values we prize more deeply than others; they become standards by which we live. The purpose of this assessment is to help you assess the values and beliefs that guide your teaching attitudes and behaviors.

PART I. Complete the following sentences:

1. I think children are generally _____

2. When children are unhappy, it's usually because _____

3. I get angry when children _____

4. The most important thing a teacher can do is _____

5. Children should not _____

6. All children are _____

7. I wish parents would _____

8. When parents _____ I feel_____

PART II. Circle the five traits and characteristics you would like children to be as a result of their preschool experience with you:

adventurous	appreciate beauty	determined
affectionate	inquisitive	energetic
polite	respectful	friendly
altruistic	self-starter	obedient
caring	sense of humor	spontaneous
honest	industrious	persistent
assertive	creative	proud
confident	independent thinker	risk-taker
cheerful	desire to excel	open-minded

From: P. J. Bloom, M. Sheerer, and J. Britz (1991). *Blueprint for Action: Achieving Center-Based Change Through Staff Development*. Published by New Horizons, PO Box 863, Lake Forest, Illinois 60045. Reprinted with permission.

Evaluating Staff Performance

A Valuable Training Tool

by Margie Carter

In teaching a child care management class and doing on-site training and consultation in early childhood programs, I've seen directors struggle to find a performance evaluation form that meets their needs. Most feel that some kind of checklist is all they have time for, yet most forms of this type aren't comprehensive enough to address all the areas of concern.

I collected scores of evaluation forms and reviewed them with directors. With their feedback I then drafted a form for them to field test.

The most significant change from the original draft to the one on the following pages is a change in the rating scale used. Originally I had columns for conventional categories such as Outstanding, Excellent, Good, Average, Poor. Directors reported that they found these too subjective and hard to distinguish.

Reinforcing the notion that we need to base evaluations on observable evidence, I then revised the form with the rating scale indicated in the key — how often this attitude and behavior is observed: Frequently, Occasionally, Never.

'Attitude' can be a subjective consideration, so it is especially important that examples that substantiate your rating be noted in the space provided. It is most useful to note specific examples with dates and descriptive details. This requires a director to be highly organized in keeping an ongoing log of teacher observations. Some have found that keeping a copy of the evaluation form in the staff member's file allows them to quickly note a periodic observation from which to later base an evaluative rating. Others just keep a single log of periodic observations of teachers and then transfer that onto evaluation forms as needed.

The following form is now widely used in the state of Washington. Many directors have a staff member use it for self-evaluation and then compare forms in their evaluation conference. The director then summarizes the discussion in the space provided, along with the identified strengths and areas for improvement. Together, the director and staff member develop and document the action plan for goals in the coming period. This is then referenced during the next evaluation cycle.

A process and form of this nature enhances the purposefulness of the evaluation process and the professionalism of those involved.

Staff Evaluation Form

Employee _____   Evaluation period ___

KEY – How often observed: F = Frequently   O = Occasionally   N = Never

General work habits	F O N
1. Arrives on time	_____
2. Reliable in attendance	_____
3. Responsible in job duties	_____
4. Alert in health and safety matters	_____
5. Follows center's philosophy	_____
6. Open to new ideas	_____
7. Flexible with assignments and schedule	_____
8. Comes to work with a positive attitude	_____
9. Looks for ways to improve the program	_____
10. Gives ample notice for absences	_____
11. Remains calm in a tense situation	_____

• Examples of behaviors observed:

_____

_____

_____

_____

_____

Attitude and skills with children	F O N
1. Friendly, warm, and affectionate	_____
2. Bends low for child-level interactions	_____
3. Uses a modulated, appropriate voice	_____
4. Shows respect for individuals	_____
5. Is aware of developmental levels/changes	_____
6. Encourages independence/self-help	_____
7. Promotes self-esteem in communications	_____
8. Limits interventions in problem solving	_____
9. Avoids stereotyping and labeling	_____
10. Reinforces positive behavior	_____
11. Minimal use of time out	_____
12. Regularly records observations of children	_____

Attitude and skills with parents	F O N
1. Available and approachable with parents	_____
2. Listens and responds well to parents	_____
3. Is tactful with negative information	_____
4. Maintains confidentiality	_____
5. Seeks a partnership with parents	_____
6. Regularly writes journal entries for parents	_____
7. Holds parent conferences on schedule	_____

• Examples of behaviors observed:

_____

_____

_____

_____

Attitude and skills with class	F O N
1. Creates an inviting learning environment	_____
2. Provides developmentally appropriate activities	_____
3. Develops plans with goals from observations	_____
4. Provides materials for all key experiences	_____
5. Provides an appropriate role model	_____
6. Anticipates problems and redirects	_____
7. Is flexible, responsive to child interests	_____
8. Is prepared for day's activities	_____
9. Handles transitions well	_____

• Examples of behaviors observed:

_____

_____

_____

_____

Attitude and skills with co-workers   **F O N**

1. Is friendly and respectful with others   _____

2. Strives to assume a fair share of work   _____

3. Offers, shares ideas and materials   _____

4. Communicates directly, avoids gossip   _____

5. Approaches criticism with learning
   attitude   _____

6. Looks for ways to be helpful   _____

• Examples of behaviors observed:

_____

_____

_____

_____

_____

Attitude and effort toward

professional development   **F O N**

1. Takes job seriously, seeks improvement   _____

2. Participates in workshops, classes,
   groups   _____

3. Reads, discusses handouts distributed   _____

4. Sets goals for self in development   _____

• Examples of behaviors observed:

_____

_____

_____

_____

**• Summary of discussion from evaluation
   conference:**

_____

_____

_____

_____

_____

• Identified strengths and leadership for center:

_____

_____

_____

_____

_____

• Goal or improvement sought for next period:

_____

_____

_____

_____

_____

• Agreed upon action plan to meet goal:

1. _____

   _____

   _____

2. _____

   _____

   _____

3. _____

   _____

   _____

Employee _____

Date _____

Supervisor _____

Date _____

Overcome the Fear of Firing

Ideas from 30 Directors

by Roger Neugebauer

> "It was obvious that this teacher could not relate well to kids, but I could not bring myself to fire her. And while I wavered, things only got worse for everyone in her classroom."

Having to fire someone is probably the most difficult action a director may have to take. It is an action directors can find endless excuses to avoid, as did the director quoted above. But it is an action that in certain cases must be taken.

To discover how directors can overcome the fear of firing and to learn what precautions to take and what mistakes to avoid in the firing process, *Exchange* surveyed 30 center directors who had fired an employee. The suggestions that follow are based on their experiences and recommendations.

When is Firing Appropriate?

People who go into social services typically care very much about individuals. However, directors are also responsible for caring for the organization as a whole and for the families it serves. When the needs of an individual staff member come into serious conflict with the needs of the group, the director must place higher priority on the welfare of the group.

The directors identified four areas where the performance of individual staff members most frequently detracts from the performance of the organization to the extent that firing may be necessary. The four areas, listed in order of frequency of occurrence, are:

Poor work habits: Chronic lateness and absenteeism; shirking of job responsibilities; sloppy, careless work. One director reported firing a teacher who "sat most of the time and shouted across the room instead of going to talk to a child. I found her sleeping in the nap room, rather than watching the nappers."

Sub-par job performance: The inability to satisfactorily perform job responsibilities; inability or unwillingness to develop necessary skills. Specific problems cited include 'lack of behavior management skills,' 'inability to supervise assistant teachers,' 'lack of empathy and patience with children,' and 'inability to plan appropriate activities.'

Unacceptable behavior: Behavior that is detrimental to children, staff, or the organization. Typically these behaviors relate to inappropriate disciplining of children such as 'striking a child,' 'verbally abusing children,' 'locking a child in the bathroom,' or 'attacking children's self-image.' Some directors also cited situations where staff members disrupted the organization by 'refusing to cooperate with other teachers,' or by 'inciting disharmony and negativism among the teachers.'

Policy violations: Unwillingness to conform to center policies and philosophies. A wide range of incidents were cited here including 'stealing center property,' 'violating the confidentiality of parent conversations,' 'refusal to adapt to the curriculum approach of the school,' and 'coming to work intoxicated.'

Potential Problems

The process of firing an employee is never a pleasant one. During the period when the director is weighing the decision and then waiting to announce it, he or she typically experiences considerable anxiety. The conference at which the employee is notified of the decision is often loaded with tension and tears, or anger and ill will. Then, if the employee reacts poorly to the action, the director may experience guilt.

Occasionally, more serious problems occur. When an employee perceives that she is being fired unjustly, she may seek to rally support among the other teachers and parents. This can lead to a period of internal conflict and leave a residue of hard feelings.

When there is a level of authority above the person who did the firing, such as an owner, a board of directors, a regional director, or a sponsoring agency, the terminated employee occasionally will appeal the decision. This appeal may proceed through normal channels such as a grievance procedure, or it may take a more personal direction. In one instance, an employee sent letters to every board member, claiming foul play by the director and demanding immediate reinstatement. In another instance, the spouse of a terminated employee appeared at the door of the center's owner threatening a lawsuit.

A confrontation may also occur if the terminated employee is denied unemployment benefits and appeals this ruling. In many states an employee who is fired may have a claim for unemployment benefits judged to be 'unapprovable' if he was fired for gross misconduct or for misdeeds directed against the employer. The information for making this decision comes from the former employer. If the former employee appeals a decision, the director may then be required to attend a hearing. One director who attended such a hearing found it very unpleasant "to be discussing the employee's poor work record in front of her, her husband, and the hearing officer."

In some cases the repercussions are even more unpleasant. Several directors reported receiving angry or obscene phone calls at home from the terminated workers for weeks; one was physically threatened. In another case, the former employee dedicated herself to spreading vicious rumors about the center and the director in the community.

Finally, a director may run the risk of incurring the ill will of other employees who may have liked the person who was fired and do not understand the reasons for dismissal. The director in these instances is in a defenseless position, since she cannot violate confidentiality by listing the reasons the person was fired. In the long run it is the credibility of the director that will lead to acceptance or non-acceptance of this decision.

Although such negative outcomes do occur, they are not inevitable. Three-fourths of the directors interviewed indicated that the positive results of firing an unsatisfactory employee far outweighed the negative ones. In most cases the morale of the staff eventually, if not immediately, improved.

Laying the Groundwork

The directors surveyed had many recommendations for avoiding the negative consequences of the firing process. Many of these had to do with laying the groundwork with actions that should be taken even before the final decision to terminate employment is made.

Establish guidelines. All personnel should know, from the day they join the center, what actions or behaviors on their part can result in their being fired. These policies should be in writing, and they should be given to all staff members or posted in a conspicuous place. Staff members have a right to know these ground rules. Once they know them, their responsibility to abide by them should not be subject to question at a termination.

Most centers spell out 'flagrant' violations that are cause for immediate termination. Cited as examples were striking a child, leaving children unattended, inflicting harsh punishments, gross negligence, and being intoxicated on the job.

Establish a grievance procedure. If at all possible, employees should have some means of appealing major personnel actions such as a firing. This may consist of a hearing before an owner, an executive director, a personnel committee, or a special grievance panel. Having such a procedure established in advance gives an aggrieved employee a clear recourse and helps prevent unnecessary parties from becoming involved in the dispute.

Review performance periodically. Once employees' performance has degenerated to the point where a termination is warranted, it may no longer be possible for them to radically alter their behavior. If the director is concerned with the welfare of individual employees and wishes to help them avoid termination, she should perform periodic performance reviews for all employees. Poor habits and sub-standard performance should be brought to the employee's attention before it gets out of hand. In these reviews, the director or supervisor should help the employee set goals for improvement as well as offer whatever support the center can muster. Progress toward meeting these goals should then be closely monitored.

Give adequate warning. Nearly every director interviewed emphasized that there should be 'no surprises.' As soon as it becomes apparent to the director that an employee may need to be fired, that employee should be warned that such an action is being considered. This warning should be given in a private conference between the director and the employee. The directors recommended that in this conference the employee should be told:

- the specific center policies the employee is violating or failing to adhere to.

- objective examples or anecdotes that demonstrate this claim.

- the specific changes required of the employee to avoid being fired.

- how the employee's effort to make these changes will be monitored.

- the deadline for the final evaluation.

Some centers have a formal two- or three-step notification process. In one center the director is required to give a preliminary verbal warning, an initial written warning, and a final written warning before issuing a notification of termination. However, if a center has an effective performance review process, the early warnings needed to give the employee a fair opportunity to improve should be coming up in the periodic reviews.

Since warning conferences can become quite emotional, key messages sometimes fail to get communicated. Sometimes directors try too hard to cushion the blow by sugarcoating the warning. In one instance, a director went to such lengths in emphasizing the employee's strong points, in addition to the problem areas, that the employee left the meeting unaware that she was close to being fired. A second message often delivered unclearly is what specific steps the employee needs to take to meet the director's expectations. To avoid miscommunication, one director suggested having the employee state his interpretation of the director's message to be sure he has an accurate understanding of it.

Keep written records. As one director urged, "Document! Document! Document!" Keep a record of periodic performance reviews, incidents of unsatisfactory performance, conferences where warnings are administered or terminations are announced. Some directors also issue warnings and terminations in writing, as well as verbally. Other directors, dealing with a particularly unstable or vindictive employee, request that the employee sign a written summary of a warning or termination conference to attest to the fact that the summary is accurate (not that they necessarily agree with it). Documentation such as this serves two purposes. First, it ensures that the director's message is conveyed. All people's memories of conversations are distorted by emotions and expectations, so it is quite likely that an employee coming out of an emotional warning conference will have a faulty memory of the specifics, unless the memory is aided by a written summary.

Second, documentation provides insurance for post-termination confrontations. If the employee challenges a firing — either before an owner, a board, or an unemployment claims officer — claiming that adequate warning was not given or that the reasons are groundless, a written record of the entire process should provide sufficient evidence to counter these claims.

Keep employers informed. Another means of avoiding potential confrontation is for the director to keep her employer up-to-date on the situation. For a director who is also the owner of the business, of course, there is no one else to turn to. However, if the director answers to a board, an owner, an executive director, a regional director, or a sponsoring agency, the appropriate party should be consulted as soon as the possibility of a termination arises. The privacy of the employee must be respected, so prior consultations should be made in confidence. One director kept the board's chairperson advised, rather than discussing the situation with the full board. When the terminated employee appealed to the board, the chairperson was able to verify the director's account of the process.

Completing the Process

Once the termination process is set in motion, a clear conclusion is necessary. Listed are the directors' recommendations for minimizing the negative effects of the final act on the employee, the director, and the organization.

Make the decision objectively. It is, of course, impossible to remove all emotion from a termination decision. How you feel about the person, how the decision will affect the individual and his family, and how it will impact the staff, all will influence the decision consciously or unconsciously. The director should not try to deny these emotions, but keep them in perspective so that they will not cause a bad decision to be made.

One way to keep issues in perspective is to avoid making a termination decision while under stress or in a crisis. When a teacher arrives 30 minutes late, thereby causing the director to miss a meeting, the director may in anger be tempted to fire the teacher on the spot. Weighing the incident later in a calmer mood, the director may realize that this was one of the few times the teacher had ever been late and that to fire her would be seriously overreacting.

Another technique for maintaining perspective is to list all the specific pieces of evidence where the employee is in fact violating center policies or failing to perform her work responsibilities. Then assess whether this list is serious enough to justify termination. If the evidence warrants termination, the director should then weigh the other negative consequences of the termination (e.g. the impact on the individual, his family, the center, the children, and the parents) to determine if the firing can be handled in such a way as to ameliorate these consequences. For example:

- Could the employee be slotted into a less demanding job in the organization?

- Could the terms of the firing be stated in such a way that the employee can receive unemployment?

- Could the employee be given an opportunity to save face by resigning first?

Another consideration at this point is setting the employee's last work day. In general, it is in everyone's best interest for the employee to leave immediately. Once the employee is fired, she may find it embarrassing to continue working at the center. In other cases, an embittered person may make life miserable for the staff or the director by stirring up trouble in the final days. In such circumstances it may be best to pay the employee severance pay for one or two weeks rather than keeping her on the job. In other cases, where feelings are less damaged, it may be helpful to allow the employee to stay on until she can find another job.

Notifying the employee. Once the termination decision has been made, the employee should be told as soon as possible in a private conference. Preferably, this should occur at the end of the day to protect the employee from confronting the other staff members when leaving. Without prolonging the agony by chit-chatting about the weather, the director should tell the employee of the decision in clear and simple terms. If this meeting has been properly prepared for, the decision should not be unexpected. Any sugarcoating or beating around the bush will only confuse the issue.

The director should state the specific reasons for the termination. There may be other unsatisfactory aspects of the employee's performance, such as sloppy dress, bad attitude, or poor relations with staff or parents; but if these are not the reasons for which the employee is being fired, they should not be mentioned in this conference. The director should also be prepared to answer all the employee's contractual questions, such as what the appeal process is, when the last day will be, whether severance pay and

unused vacation time will be granted, and whether the director will write a job recommendation for the employee in the future. All important points should, of course, be included in a termination letter given to the employee during the conference.

In certain circumstances the director may be inclined to offer the employee help in applying for benefits or in finding a new job. This fact should be stated, but the director should not press to offer help unless the employee specifically asks for it.

Announce the action honestly. The other employees, and in some cases the parents, will have an extreme interest in the action. If they are not informed, eventually the rumor mill will begin generating distorted versions of what happened. Such rumors can have a negative impact on staff morale and staff-director relations. Therefore, the staff and parents should be informed about the termination as soon as possible and as honestly as possible, without violating the former employee's privacy by revealing details.

If the employee was popular among the staff and parents, they may find fault with the decision. But the director should not attempt to regain their approval by revealing confidential information or by reversing the decision. More likely than not, however, staff members will be more relieved than angered by the decision. Twenty-eight of the 30 directors reported that staff members reacted positively to termination decisions.

No one enjoys firing an employee, and firings seldom go without some trauma. But to maintain the integrity of the program for the children, the staff, and the parents, such actions may be necessary. And, if handled properly, the negative repercussions can be minimized.

Roger Neugebauer

Roger Neugebauer is publisher of *Exchange Magazine* and a co-founder of the World Forum Foundation.

.

the Art of
LEADERSHIP
DEVELOPING
PEOPLE IN
EARLY CHILDHOOD ORGANIZATIONS

4 CHAPTER 4
Promoting Teamwork

All the Teachers are Friends Here *by Nancy Rosenow* 104

Ten Strategies for Coaching a Winning Team *by Pam Schiller* 108

Step-by-Step Guide to Team Building *by Roger Neugebauer* 112

Using the Rules of Improvisation to Build Playful Teams *by Kelly Matthews* 119

Learning to Play Well with Others *by Jeny Searcy* 125

Indicators of Effective Teamwork *by Margie Carter* 129

When Friction Flares: Dealing with Staff Conflict *by Roger Neugebauer* 134

Ten Teamwork Terminators and Some Cures *by Hawaii Directors Network attendees* 139

All the Teachers are Friends Here

The Case for Strong Relationships Among Adults Who Work with Young Children

by Nancy Rosenow

Walking into the early childhood program I've been associated with for over 30 years, I overheard the following conversation between three-year-old Abby and her mother, Susan.

Abby: "Look, there's Mrs. Miller."

Susan: "How do you know her?"

Abby: "She's a friend of my teacher. Mom, don't you know that all the teachers are friends here?"

What a profound statement! It stopped me in my tracks. I thought about the kinds of things we adults unwittingly convey to children every day. If Abby, at age three, can sense the strong and (mostly) positive relationships among staff members on our team, then it's just as likely she can sense when there's tension and unease. And, when human beings work together, there will inevitably be times when relationships feel challenging. In staff's efforts to make positive connections among coworkers a valued goal, children learn how to form positive relationships by example. That's why continuity of staff is so important, and something that lately I fear may be disregarded. Consider the following recent experiences:

- Maria is the principal of an early childhood program in a large public school system. For the past year she and her staff worked tirelessly to transform a hardscape playground into a natural outdoor classroom. Teachers shared ideas, involved families, connected with the local community, then everyone came together to celebrate a 'grand opening.' I was there to rejoice with Maria. However, when I congratulated her, she responded with a subdued shrug. "Well," she replied softly, "I won't be around to enjoy it with my team. The district wants to move me to a 'failing' school so I can do it all over again."

- Henry works at an elementary school in a challenging area. Visiting recently, I told him how much our team enjoyed the workshops we've been holding with his staff, and what a cohesive group he's put together. "Those days are coming to an end," he told me. "Our superintendent doesn't like it when a staff becomes too close. He thinks it leads to problems. He likes to shake things up by moving folks around."

- Carol is the director of a community-based early childhood center that cares for infants and toddlers. She is dealing with the effects of a depressed local economy and her board of directors wants to cut teacher salaries to offset decreased tuition revenues. "I'm so afraid we'll lose some of our best teachers if we do this," Carol told me sadly. "Our board just doesn't understand how important it is to keep our staff intact."

When I think about what Maria, Henry, and Carol are facing, it would be awfully easy for me to decry 'the impersonal system' or the 'unfeeling administration'; but that is not helpful, and likely unfair. My guess is there might be a lack of understanding about just how crucial staff continuity is to a child care program or elementary school. Recent research (from both the early childhood field and the business world) provides compelling evidence that continuity of staff is good not only for children, but for adults as well. Best-selling authors James Kouzes and Barry Posner (2010), in their recent book, *The Truth about Leadership*, discuss how important it is for people who run organizations to have time to get to know their staff on a personal level. They quote a study from the Center for Creative Leadership that identified the critical success factor for leaders is 'relationships with subordinates.' In the case of Maria, who was quite successful in forming relationships with teachers, parents, and community members, the urge to send her to a struggling school in hopes she could 'work her magic' again is understandable. It's also unfortunate, and flies in the face of what we know about how healthy organizations work.

Kouzes and Posner (2010) discuss the importance of giving leaders the time and continuity of staff needed to create trusting, positive relationships. They write, "The mandate is very clear. Build your own and your team members' abilities to work with each other. Doing this well will have a direct impact on your personal and organizational success." A common misconception, perhaps reflected by the superintendent Henry works for, is that too much familiarity among staff can lead to problems. And Carol told me that her board members feel that 'adding new blood' will be a good thing for the program. While this may be true in some ways, losing experienced teachers will not be positive. Is it possible to maximize the benefits of longevity of staff while minimizing some of the possible negative effects?

Carolyn Duff (1993) wrote a book called *When Women Work Together*. It's based on surveys with over 500 women to find what works and what doesn't in building strong relationships among female-dominated staff. Her findings may be helpful to the early childhood field, since women still represent a high percentage of our staff (although admirable efforts are underway to encourage more men to join the profession).

Listed are a few guiding principles from Duff's research (1993) and other sources:

Make time for creating personal connections a priority. Just as Kouzes and Posner (2010) report, Duff (1993) also found that building positive working relationships takes time. When staff experience constant turnover, or if people are moved from place-to-place within an organization like interchangeable pieces on a chess board, morale falls and relationships stay at surface level at best. Duff says that "relationship networks don't just happen. They grow from trust and our knowing and connecting with each other." She suggests that to optimize relationships, leaders should encourage people to share personal stories at the beginning of staff meetings or through staff newsletters. Rather than wasting time, these chances to connect help make the whole organization run more effectively.

Work hard to avoid 'us and them' feelings. One potential pitfall that staff who have been together for years sometimes face is a reluctance to accept new people or new ideas. One solution is for leaders to encourage honest discussion and healthy debate on a regular basis. People might be encouraged to reconsider long-held beliefs, with some staff playing the role of 'devil's advocate' during the discussion. Even if at the end of the debate the consensus is that the belief still rings true, the fact that new ways of looking at the world have been encouraged will guard against the "we've always done it that way" mentality. It's also important to be honest about the loss people sometimes feel when a long-time staff member leaves and a new person takes her place. When leaders acknowledge these feelings and allow them to be expressed, while also clearly communicating the expectation that the new person will be welcomed and embraced, then healing can take place and new relationships can flourish.

Carefully solicit people's input before decisions are made. Especially among staff who have been together for a long time, leaders need to be intentional about continuing to involve everyone in decision making as much as possible. It can be too easy to fall into the trap of presuming to know how people think, without actually stopping to check. Even if regular staff meetings are not always possible, written surveys to solicit ideas and reactions to proposals can be quite helpful. Leaders need to make it clear that once all input has been carefully considered, staff members need to abide by and support the final decision. People are usually willing to do so if they know their thoughts have been heard.

Learn to communicate without taking it personally. The flip side of close positive relationships among staff can be a tendency to invest too emotionally in the job. As Duff (1993) says, it can become counterproductive when people "give personal meaning to every work situation. They get their feelings hurt too easily. They're too touchy. They spend more time reacting than working." Leaders can minimize this tendency by serving as good role models for how to handle situations that might lead to 'hurt feelings.' In his book, *Creating Passion-driven Teams,* Dan Bobinski (2009), a director at the Center for Workplace Excellence, encourages leaders to talk to staff about the difference between disagreement, tension, and conflict. Disagreements are a part of life and are to be expected. It's important to help people understand how disagreements can be expressed and heard in a positive way without 'taking it personally.' When disagreements are consistently placed on the table for discussion, with all issues fair game, Bobinski defines this as healthy conflict. When conflict is suppressed and kept unspoken, Bobinski defines this as tension. The leader's goal should be to encourage and teach healthy conflict resolution, while discouraging unhealthy tension among people.

Admit mistakes. In a closely connected staff, just like in a close-knit family, people make mistakes. Healthy staff are most able to admit and forgive mistakes if their leader feels comfortable doing so. As Kouzes and Posner (2010) say:

"Leaders make mistakes, mess up, and speak out on occasions when they should keep their mouths shut. Like the rest of us, leaders are only human…. Nothing undermines or erodes your credibility and your effectiveness as a role model faster than not being willing to take responsibility when you've made a mistake."

This advice hit home for me recently when I needed to apologize to my staff and clear the air of misunderstandings. Because of our shared history and close connections with each other, we were able to talk openly about my 'opportunity for growth' (as we've decided to think of our mistakes). I wondered how easy it would have been for me to have similar conversations with a constantly changing staff. I'm glad I won't have to find out.

Finally, it's important to remember the adverse effects that 'shaking things up by moving people around' have on young children. An article about infants and toddlers on the Zero to Three website (Lally, Torres, & Phelps, 1993) reminds us that:

"Switching from one caregiver to another takes its toll. The child has to build trust all over again. When a very young child loses a caregiver, he really loses part of his sense of himself and the way the world operates. Too many changes in caregivers can lead to a child's reluctance to form new relationships."

I hope Carol will communicate this fact to her board of directors. And I hope anyone who makes decisions about staff continuity will ponder carefully the immense benefits that are possible when 'all the teachers are friends.'

References

Bobinski, D. (2009). *Creating passion-driven teams: How to stop micromanaging and motivate people to top performance.* Franklin Lakes, NJ: Career Press.

Duff, C. (1993). *When women work together: Using our strengths to overcome our challenges.* Berkeley, CA: Conari Press.

Kouzes, J,. & Posner, B. (2010). *The truth about leadership: The no-fads, heart-of-the-matter facts you need to know.* San Francisco, CA: Jossey-Bass.

Lally, J. R., Torres, Y. L., & Phelps, P. C. (1993). "Caring for infants and toddlers in groups." Washington, DC: Zero to Three Press. Retrieved from www.zerotothree.org/early-care-education/child-care-education/child-care/caring-for-infant-and-toddlers-in-groups.html

Nancy Rosenow

Nancy Rosenow is the executive director of Dimensions Educational Research Foundation/Nature Explore and a founding member of World Forum Foundation's Nature Action Collaborative for Children.

Ten Strategies for Coaching a Winning Team

by Pam Schiller

A successful director is in many ways like a winning coach. Both encourage people to work together. Both inspire people to do their best. Both are boosters of morale. A director who carefully selects a team and practices effective coaching skills will create a high-quality environment for both children and staff.

We have all witnessed cases where a team of talented baseball players just can't seem to have a winning season. Each player is outstanding individually, but the cooperative effort just doesn't create the desired result. Then a new coach is hired and, bingo, everything comes together.

A good coach is able to see how each person's strength fortifies the team and is able to bring those skills and talents into consort. With this kind of leadership, the whole team benefits and each individual player is able to blossom to full potential.

Be a Good Scout

Building a winning team begins with the selection of the players. A good coach is a good scout. Looking for the right players for the right positions in the beginning will save time and energy in the long run. It gives the team an early advantage.

Make a list of attributes you expect to find in an employee and stay committed to not settling for less. Ask prospective candidates why they want the job. This information in all actuality will determine to what extent the candidate will be an asset to your team. Answers like "I'm not trained for other work" or "I figure anyone can watch children" aren't acceptable. You are looking for team members who enjoy children and have a passion for making a difference in their lives. You want team members who believe they can make a difference. You want people who believe they are the best candidates for the job.

Hire people who are versatile. Versatility provides flexibility. On a playing field or in a child care center, flexibility is an advantage. In a pinch, you may need the assistant director to cover the two-year-old room or the cook to accompany children on a field trip.

Ask yourself if the candidate fits into the existing team. Will this player get along with others? Will she be committed to the good of the whole? Does she enhance the team as a whole?

Finding the right players is only the first step in building the team. Placing them in the right positions is equally important. Before placing new team members, evaluate their talents, capabilities, inadequacies, needs, and wants. Ask about preferences for age groups and working schedules. Listening closely will enable you to make the best match between a team member's strengths and desires and available positions on the team.

Let Orientation be Your Warm Up

Start with the end in mind. Plan an orientation for team members that allow them to know exactly what your expectations are. Provide copies of rules and policies and discuss and give examples of each. An employee needs to know in advance that you expect caregivers to space themselves on the playground instead of huddling together talking to each other.

Employees should not have to find out about a rule by breaking it. If your employees understand what the rules are and why they exist (in the example above, spreading out on the playground helps prevent accidents), they are much more likely to develop good habits from the beginning.

In addition to rules and responsibilities, discuss personnel policies. Outline your center's structure, methods of communications, personal space, policies regarding promotion, and probationary periods.

Establish a 30-day period during which you and the new team member have a scheduled time set aside to discuss progress. Your goal is to coach your new team member to be the best she can be in her new position. This takes time and practice. Perfect practice means the team member receives feedback on her progress and is allowed time for self-evaluation.

Offer a Training Camp

Training is critical to maintaining the team in body, mind, and spirit. Initial training helps a new team member get off on the right foot, while continual training keeps everyone on the right foot and also builds camaraderie and morale.

Assign new team members a mentor. We typically use this strategy for helping new children learn the ropes and feel more at ease. Why not our staff?

Provide an opportunity for new employees to actually work beside someone in a comparable job for a day or two. This is absolutely one of the best strategies you can use to boost a new team member's confidence and understanding of expectations. It allows him to walk in the footsteps of someone doing the job well.

Be sure to think of ways to reward your mentors. Don't fall into the trap of thinking that just being selected as a mentor is reward enough. It may not seem that way at all to your mentor. Use more concrete and visible rewards like a gift certificate, an extra break, or getting to go home early one day.

Make staff training for your whole team a regular routine. You want to keep staff inspired with new ideas and motivated toward constant improvement. Plan in-house training and, whenever possible, use the talents of staff. Ask Sam to demonstrate his art ideas and Tiffany to show the movement activities she uses on rainy days.

Use spontaneous training. Occasionally surprise your staff with special supplies for a new activity. Place the supplies in the workroom with a sign: Make, Take, and Try!

Make training accessible and fun whenever possible. When professional workshops are given in the community, offer to drive the facility van. Get team members together for breakfast before the workshop starts or for lunch between sessions.

Get Your Signals Straight

Communication is key to the game. You need clear, direct, two-way communication between you and the team, you and the families in the center, the team and the families, and the team and the children. A competent coach will constantly think of ways to improve communication because clear communication means that everyone stays on track. It also is at the heart of team member and fan morale.

Establish regular and frequent communication. Plan for general communication by means of bulletin boards, staff newsletters, and staff meetings. Plan for personal communication through individual mailboxes.

Involve the team in communication when possible. A staff or parent newsletter can be more than an administrative memo from the director. It can include contributions from staff or parents.

Remember that our actions speak louder than our words. Treat all team members equally. What applies to one applies to all.

Provide your team members with appropriate support for communicating effectively with parents. Practice possible daily scenarios so that everyone knows automatically what to do when challenges appear. Give players a playbook. Set up responses to daily scenarios and parent comments and concerns that provide solutions and responses for staff to follow. For example, provide a response in the playbook for what to say to a parent who is concerned about a biter in their child's classroom or the length of naptime. Practice these responses.

Use a Visible Scoreboard

Recognize individual staff members through daily activities and in program planning. Visit each classroom when you arrive in the morning and greet each staff member by name.

Highlight each team member's personal and professional accomplishments. Use staff memo, parent newsletter, or bulletin board display to acknowledge Madison's unique bulletin board, Gabrielle's completion of a first aid course, and Tamera's new grandmother status. To emphasize the individual's importance to the team effort, display a *Who's Who on the Team* or a Hall of Fame photo gallery of all team members.

Treat team members with empathy when personal challenges arise. If you can adjust the work schedule while Judy's husband is in the hospital, do so. Invite staff to help think of ways to fill in for Judy. Pick up the slack yourself when possible. These actions create a climate of caring essential to team building.

Recognize longevity and loyalty with a progression of awards. People who complete one year of employment may get a day off. After two years, they may get a designated parking space. For extensive longevity, consider naming a room after the employee. The yellow room can just as easily be called Ms. Joan's Room or the kitchen Alice's Place.

Consult the Team

Actively solicit input from your team. It is a true statement about human behavior that what we help build, we are far more likely to support.

Involve staff in the decision-making processes of the center. When money is available for equipment or supplies, ask for staff input on how to spend it. Staff members are far more likely to recognize that a new tricycle will help avoid more conflict on the playground than a new jungle gym.

Involve staff in setting policy. Classroom teachers, for example, may recognize that a particular policy regarding show-and-tell is disruptive to the class schedule and should be changed. This kind of staff involvement not only improves the caring environment, but also contributes to a 'we' feeling in the center. Being involved as a decision maker allows each person to know she has some control over her work environment.

Stay Focused

Coaching is continuous. A coach watches the team no matter what other stress is around. It is the coach's job to remove a tired player, see a nervous pitcher, watch for frustration, and so forth. The coach does this even though the general manager is making demands, the score is behind, the fans are asking for autographs, and a team member is injured.

Employees get frustrated, isolated, and overwhelmed. It is the director's role to recognize these situations and intercede before they become insurmountable or threatening to the health of the team.

Remember the Seventh-inning Stretch

Recognize the social needs of the team. Working in child care is one of the most stressful jobs a person can have. Breaks are essential for reducing stress and for allowing adults opportunities to communicate with other adults. Staff members need a quiet and comfortable place to relax and refuel. Providing for a few minutes away ensures staff members return to the classroom more patient and loving.

Plan for staff socials in recognition of birthdays, holidays, graduations, engagements, and other special events. Bring-a-dish meals or bring-an-ingredient salad luncheons are excellent ways of encouraging social interactions. Everyone deserves a celebration and a stretch every once in a while.

Be a Model

Be a model of the behavior you expect from the team. Treat parents with respect. Offer to help when a caregiver wants to rearrange her room. Share your ideas, talents, and materials. Be friendly to everyone. Be willing to do anything you ask your staff to do.

Some centers have established core values — a code by which to live and work. Core values provide clear objectives and focus for all employees. They also send a strong message to parents and the community about the center's goals. Children's World Learning Centers has developed a set of core values. These values dictate the expected behaviors of everyone from the CEO to the assistant teacher in each classroom. Their values are:

■ Do the right thing.

■ Make a difference.

■ Keep your promises.

■ Help each other.

Create Raving Fans

One of the most visible signs of a winning team is loyal and dedicated fans. Who are your fans? They are the children and families you serve. Your ultimate goal is to have children who can't wait to return to your center the next day and families who can't wait to recommend your center to their friends.

The best way for you to create those raving fans is to build and coach a winning team. Team members will blossom with the support of raving fans and so will the coach.

You don't have to win the World Series to have a winning team. You just have to play your best game every time you are on the field. How does this happen in child care? By creating a team with high morale, one that communicates well, practices, and remains dedicated to the passion to create a happy, secure, loving, and challenging environment for children.

Pam Schiller

Pam Schiller, Ph.D., is senior national early childhood consultant for SRA/McGraw-Hill, and past president of the Southern Early Childhood Association. She was the administrator of a child care center for several years and has also taught in the public schools as a kindergarten teacher. She is senior author of *The DLM Early Childhood Program*, a full curriculum for preschool children, as well as a number of teacher resource books.

Step-by-Step Guide to Team Building

by Roger Neugebauer

According to management consultant Peter F. Drucker, the team concept of management is ideally suited to a knowledge organization — an organization that trades in ideas, concepts, and services. Such an organization — and an early childhood center clearly falls into this category — can extract maximum performance from its workers by managing them as important players on a team, rather than as faceless members of the staff.

Recognizing the potential value of a team approach to the management of an early childhood organization, this article describes a step-by-step process for building an effective team.

Developing a staff of individuals into an effectively functioning team can be a rewarding experience. When a staff is functioning as a team, team members' interrelationships can be supportive, satisfying, and stimulating. Team members will be motivated and enabled to use their talents to the fullest.

Unfortunately, team building is not a quick and painless process. In fact, a center should not even consider making the effort to engage in team building unless all participants are aware of how it will affect them:

- For the leader (whether this is the director, a coordinator, or a head teacher), this means being willing to delegate a considerable amount of authority to the team, being patient when it initially takes the team longer to accomplish a certain task than it would for you on your own, and being able to accept that not everything is going to be done your way. For the leader, it means functioning more as a facilitator than as a boss.

- For subordinates, this means being willing to accept some leadership responsibilities, being more concerned with the interests of the team than with your own interests, and being able to be open and caring in your relationships with other team members. For subordinates, this means functioning as an active participant in the process, rather than as a passive follower of orders.

The Team-building Process

The team-building process described below is designed specifically for the early childhood setting. Built into it is the assumption that the organization is strapped for time and resources — that staff members do not have a lot of free time to devote to process, and that the organization cannot afford to send the entire staff away for weeks at a time to engage in team-building exercises.

In addition, it takes into account the probability that, at the outset, staff members will be unwilling and unable to jump right in and assume significant levels of responsibility.

As a result, the following five-step process is designed to be implemented gradually and flexibly. It can be carried out over a period of months as part of regular weekly staff meetings. It can allow various staff members to participate at varying levels of responsibility. And it provides a check to make sure that everyone is satisfied with how the process is working.

Step #1 — Set achievable goals

According to Troy D. Bussey, having clear goals is the key factor to team effectiveness. "Mutually agreed upon goals," he observes, "constitute a cohesive and energizing force for all members of the team."

To have this energizing force, the goals should meet these criteria:

- They should be understood and accepted by all team members. The best way to make this happen is to have all team members participate in the goal-setting process. One technique for doing this is High Participation Goal Setting (see box).

- They should be challenging, yet achievable. If goals are too difficult to achieve, team members will soon give up trying, and their motivational force will be lost. Likewise, if goals are too easily accomplished, there will not be much challenge.

- They should be measurable. If at all possible, the team's general goals should be translated into specific yardsticks against which progress can be measured. For example, the goal: *To instill a cooperative spirit in children* could be specified as: *To increase the incidence of cooperative play by 25%.*

High Participation Goal Setting

When attempting to involve all team members in the goal-setting process, the most skilled and most assertive team members may tend to dominate the process. If this is likely to happen in your center, you may want to consider employing a variation of the Delphi Technique to set goals. This technique assures that all individuals have an opportunity to get their views before the team. The process works as follows:

- Have each member of the team anonymously write down what they believe should be the top two or three goals of the center.

- Read through all these statements, eliminate duplicates, and compile them into a single list.

- Circulate this list back to all team members with the instructions that they select from this list their recommendations for the top three center goals.

- Count how many times each goal is selected and then present the top three or four vote getters to the team at the next staff meeting. At this meeting, team members should discuss these potential goals, agree on which ones make sense to tackle at the same time, and make suggestions as to how these might be stated more clearly.

- Write up the agreed upon goals based on the comments in the meeting and pass these statements out to team members for their final review.

- At the next staff meeting, make final revisions and formally approve the goals. Write up the approved goals and distribute copies to all team members.

■ They should have diverse time frames. Especially at the outset of the team-building process, there should be one or two goals that can be achieved within a short period of time, such as: *To redesign the toddler room so as to reduce the noise level.* By achieving some goals fairly quickly, individuals will be more inclined than ever to work together as a team to achieve its long-term objectives.

Step #2 — Clarify roles

Team members work most effectively together when their roles are clear and reasonably free of conflict. Ideally, each team member should know what tasks she is responsible for, as well as what tasks each other member is responsible for.

An opportune time to clarify roles is just after going through the goal-setting process. At this point, there should be some sense of excitement about embarking on a new venture. Team members should be more open than normal to reexamining and redefining their roles.

To clarify roles at this point, team members first should brainstorm about all the areas of responsibility that the team must assume if it is to accomplish its new goals. For example, team members may list such things as…

■ developing daily plans.

■ developing curriculum activities.

■ redesigning the classroom.

■ selecting curriculum materials.

■ buying curriculum materials.

■ cleaning up the classroom.

■ supervising student teachers.

After the list is completed, each area of responsibility will need to be formally assigned to one or more team members. The more team members participate in this assignment process, the more accepting they are likely to be of the final breakdown. In any event,

the team leader will need to exercise final judgment in cases where team members can't agree, or in cases where team members, due to their inexperience, are biting off more than they can chew.

In addition to these formal roles relating to the accomplishment of team goals, there also exists an entirely different set of informal roles. These roles relate to the internal functioning of the team. For example, in order for a team to function well, someone on the team needs to accept responsibility for harmonizing relationships among staff members, for encouraging less assertive or experienced team members to participate actively, and for initiating action when a problem or opportunity exists.

While it does not make sense to assign these roles formally, the team leader should continually monitor team functioning to be sure that all necessary roles are being performed by someone.

Step #3 — Build supportive relationships

At the beginning of each year, Clare Cherry challenged each of her teachers to see to it that each of the other teachers had the best year teaching that they'd ever had (Cherry). This type of cooperative spirit is exactly what is needed to make a team work. In an effectively functioning team, each team member draws strength from the personal satisfaction of being a part of a caring group of individuals, as well as from the professional support provided by team members.

However, it is very easy to say that team members should care about each other and support each other, but it is not so easy to make this happen. While the team leader cannot require team members to be supportive, she can structure situations that encourage this to happen, and she can remove obstacles that often prevent it. Listed are examples of approaches that some directors have found effective:

■ **Feedback training.** In a survey of child care centers in New England, "lack of feedback on my performance" was identified by teachers as their greatest frustration (Neugebauer, 1975). The same teachers indicated that the persons they most would respect feedback from are the teachers they work with. Unfortunately, teachers often lack the skills and inclination to give useful feedback. To stimulate the flow of feedback among teachers, it may be helpful to provide training to teachers on how to give effective feedback.

■ **Team resource people.** Betty Jones has observed that it is easy for a director to view herself as the final authority on everything, when in fact in many areas there are other staff members who know more than she does (Jones). To tap the expertise that exists among team members and to get team members into the habit of looking to each other for support instead of always relying on the team leader, some centers have found it helpful to designate different members of the team as resource persons for specific topics, such as music, large motor skills, aggression, or language. These people will be designated on the basis of their current skills and interests, and they will be expected to do some extra research to keep up to date.

■ **Best-worst incidents.** In a team where there is not yet a great deal of trust and openness, it may be difficult for team members to know enough about the needs and feelings of their peers to provide them support. One approach many centers use to encourage team members to open up is the *best-worst incidents* approach. At a team meeting, the leader asks each staff member to relate the best thing that happened to her at the center the past week, as well as the worst thing.

An infinite number of variations on this theme could be used: What is the toughest problem you have solved this week and the toughest you have yet to solve? What parent comment made you feel best this week and which one made you feel worst? Not only does this technique give all team members an easy way to share their victories and receive some positive

strokes, it also gives other team members ideas on how they can provide some support.

Step #4 — Encourage active participation

One of the positive features of the team approach to management is that it can take maximum advantage of the abilities and knowledge of individual team members. However, this utilization of member resources does not happen automatically. A team leader needs to be resourceful in encouraging all team members to contribute their ideas, opinions, and energies. Listed are some suggestions:

■ **Spotlight challenges.** The creative talents of a team are more likely to be unleashed if there is a specific task to focus on (Uris). The team leader can stimulate team members by pointing out a specific problem that is of major concern to the center (the frequency of accidents on the climbing structure) or an opportunity of high potential (the growing demand for drop-in care in the community).

■ **Provide a fertile environment.** Creativity seldom involves the creation of a totally new idea. Organizational theorist James March has observed that "most innovations in an organization are a result of borrowing rather than invention." Put another way, creativity involves combining conventional ideas in unconventional ways. Therefore, the team leader should ensure that team members have rich and varied experiences to draw upon. This would involve such steps as providing a wealth of reading materials in the teachers' lounge, encouraging team members to visit other centers, and making it possible for them to attend classes and workshops.

■ **Demonstrate interest.** Nothing kills the enthusiasm of individuals in developing a new idea more quickly than the realization that no one else is interested in it. If one or more team members are working on a new room arrangement, parent communication form, or nap time routine, the team leader should support their efforts by demonstrating an interest in what they are doing, as well as by bringing it to the attention of the entire team.

■ **Offer help when needed.** Not all individuals have an equal ability to come up with an inspiration, to flesh it out, and to develop it into a ready-to-implement product. A team leader needs to be sensitive to the creative styles of various team members. She needs to be able to jump in and offer a helping hand to those who can only come up with gleam-in-the-eye-stage ideas, while standing aside and letting others run their ideas through to completion (Uris).

■ **Foster a permissive atmosphere.** All team members need to feel that their ideas and contributions are welcomed and valued. The team leader needs to nurture a climate in the team that is accepting of new ideas — no matter how outlandish they may initially appear.

Spiro Agnew loudly decried the *instant analyses* of television news commentators. While one may suspect that he was more upset by the content of their analyses than their speed, his concern does highlight the discouraging aspect of immediate critical reaction. If a team member lacks confidence or assertiveness to begin with, he will certainly be doubly reluctant to expose his ideas to the team if he knows they will be criticized, ridiculed, or ignored.

That is not to say, of course, that all ideas should be accepted no matter what. Certainly every proposal should be subject to careful, objective scrutiny by the team before implementation. However, such a critical examination should only take place after the contributor has had the opportunity to explain it fully, and even try it out if possible.

■ **Allow for individual interests.** According to organizational psychologist Harry Levinson, an organization is best served when it "permits people to seize and develop those challenges that most excite their curiosity." In spotlighting challenges for the team, the team leader should not restrict attention to a single problem, but should delineate a wide range of opportunities for useful innovation. Being able to follow one's interest is more likely to stimulate a flow of ideas than being restricted to a problem that is critical, but of little interest.

Step #5 — Monitor team effectiveness

You can't build a house without occasionally stepping back to see if all the workers' efforts are resulting in a solid, saleable product. Likewise, you can't build a team without periodically monitoring to determine if progress is being made.

Two types of monitoring are of value. First and foremost, the team should be evaluated in terms of whether it is accomplishing its goals. It can be very rewarding for team members when they see that their cooperative efforts are really making a difference. This can provide all the more incentive to work hard at making the team work. Conversely, it is vital for team members to know as soon as possible if their efforts are not moving them closer to the accomplishment of their goals. The sooner they know their efforts are misdirected, the less time they will waste before making necessary corrections.

Monitoring progress against goals, or program evaluation, can take many forms. Ideally, the team should be able to express its goals in measurable terms so that there can be some direct yardstick of progress. For example, a team's goal might be expressed as *reducing incidents of aggressive behavior by 30%*. At the beginning of the year, someone could observe the number of incidents of aggression occurring in a classroom over a set period of time. Then, every two or three months, a similar count could be made to see if the number of incidents of aggression is actually declining.

More often than not, however, goals in early childhood settings are not measurable. In these cases, the team must rely on less direct indicators of progress — parent satisfaction surveys, comparisons of behavioral descriptions from diaries, period observations by outside consultants, and the like. While such techniques may not yield any cut-and-dried indications of progress, they can provide team members with significant amounts of helpful feedback.

The second type of monitoring that a team can and should engage in is the assessment of team functioning. At least two or three times a year, team members should take time out to assess how well they are working together as a team. The longer the gap between assessments, the more likely it is that minor shortcomings will degenerate into major problems.

Monitoring of team functioning need not be a complex process. Typically, what happens is that team members anonymously rate the team using a checklist of functions and then discuss the findings and their implications at a team meeting.

As can be seen from the preceding discussion, getting a team approach launched and up to speed is not a simple process. It requires time, patience, and the willingness of all involved to open themselves up to new ways of working and relating to each other. However, in a profession that demands so much creativity, so much flexibility, and so much in terms of interpersonal skills, the team approach offers an excellent vehicle for achieving peak performance.

References and Resources

Bussey, T. D. (1984, January/February). "Building a Winning Team." *Nonprofit World Report.*

Cherry, C. (1991). "Promoting Harmonious Staff Relationships." *Fostering improved staff performance.* Redmond, WA: Exchange Press.

Common Team Problems

Role ambiguity. Sometimes certain areas of responsibility are left out in never-never land. Everyone knows that they exist, but no one knows whose responsibility they are. This often happens with menial responsibilities that nobody wants to touch, such as cleaning up the classroom at the end of the day and keeping the book and toy shelves well organized. Sometimes it can occur with very important tasks that are hard to find time for. Everyone on the team may believe that researching new ideas or evaluating the curriculum are important, but if no one is specifically charged with carrying out these tasks, they just don't get done.

Role conflict. Conflict can occur when two or more team members believe they have responsibility for the same task. A teacher and a director may both believe that it is their responsibility to bring a major concern with a child to the attention of his parents. When this occurs, both team members may end up expending a considerable amount of energy outwardly arguing about whose job it is, or inwardly dealing with anger and frustration. This energy drained off unproductively into the conflict is energy that could more profitably be invested in accomplishing the team's goals.

Intergroup conflict. Conflict can also occur between groups of individuals (i.e., between teams). If the staff of a center is divided into two teams, one serving the preschool children and one serving the infants and toddlers, these two teams may come into conflict over the use of space, over money for supplies, or over use of the kitchen facilities. This is a behavior that very often occurs in the early stages of team building in larger organizations. Team members become so loyal to their own team that anyone on the outside is looked upon as a competitor. This we-they attitude is encouraging to the extent that it shows that some esprit de corps is beginning to develop among team members. However, in its extreme form, it can be harmful to the organization as a whole.

Drucker, P. F. (1973). *Management*. New York: Harper & Row, Publishers.

Jones, E. (1990). "Creating Environments Where Teachers, Like Children, Learn Through Play." In *Developing staff skills*. Redmond, WA: Exchange Press.

Levinson, H. (1968). *The exceptional executive*. Cambridge, MA: Harvard University Press.

March, J., & Simon, H. (1958). *Organizations*. New York: John Wiley and Sons.

Neugebauer, R. (1983, November). "Assessing Team Performance." *Exchange Magazine*.

Neugebauer, R. (1991). "Guidelines for Effective Use of Feedback." *Exchange Magazine*.

Neugebauer, R. (1991). "How to Stimulate Creativity in Your Staff." *Exchange Magazine*.

Neugebauer, R. (1975). "Organizational Analysis of Day Care." Arlington, VA: ERIC Document Reproduction Service.

Uris, A. (1976). *The executive deskbook*. New York: Van Nostrand Reinhold Company.

Roger Neugebauer

Roger Neugebauer is publisher of *Exchange Magazine* and a co-founder of the World Forum Foundation.

Using the Rules of Improvisation to Build Playful Teams

by Kelly Matthews

"Real life isn't scripted.
Neither is real teaching."

Debbie Miller, *Teaching with Intention*

The shelves abound with team-building books. Titles like *The Ten-Minute Inservice*[28] and *Quick Team Building Activities for Busy Managers*[17] inspire directors to plan snappy activities to encourage positive staff relationships. From "Toolboxes" to "Strategies" to "Activity Guides," ideas overflow. But what would happen if we looked at something deeper? What if we focused on dispositions? Dispositions are contrasted with discrete skills; they've been described as 'habits of mind,'[6] which can be taught or strengthened.

The world of improvising may seem like an unlikely source of inspiration, but the 'habits of mind' that improv troupes follow as a way of being with their fellow players make a lot of sense in the early childhood world. While Sawyer's work documenting the intersection of early childhood education and improvisation dealt mostly with teacher-student interactions or child-to-child interactions,[20-26] Lobman's research[7-14] examines how supporting teachers through improvisational means impacts teaching. I am inspired by their work and further ask: What might early childhood programs learn from exploring improvisational ideas and 'rules' to get the most out of our professional teaching staff and administration?

What are these improvisational ideas? We may have some familiarity with improv ideas through exposure to shows like "Whose Line is it Anyway?" or having visited comedy troupes like Second City. Generalized definitions of improvisation often include sentiments like 'being in the moment,' 'making things up,' 'being spontaneous,' or 'making do with what you have'.[3] But as you will see, these tenets remind us that good improvisation doesn't 'just happen'; dispositions that support flexibility, seeing multiple perspectives, and openness are needed. Which is all to say, being 'in the moment' is a lot of work if done correctly.

These 'rules,' ironic as that idea may be when thinking about improvisation, help players know what to expect, even when creating the unexpected. They are teachable[2, 9, 15] and have been generally accepted by troupes as their working agreements. These tenets, found in several of the improv 'handbooks'[4, 15, 19] include, but are not limited to:

- making offers.

- accepting/blocking.

- yes, and….

■ in the moment — improv style.

■ team scene/do not play-write.

■ be a good player.

■ be comfortable with possibility.

Making Offers

In the world of improv, an offer is "anything that any-one says or does in a story or scene."[9] This may seem like an expansive definition, but given that good players use everything available to them, it makes perfect sense.

In child care, we see children make offers all the time to each other; each time a child holds out a block and defines it as something else to start the play, we've seen an offer in action. As adults, our offers are more subtle, taking the form of body posture, the ideas we share at meetings, or deciding to try something new. Making and accepting offers are the building blocks of all good improv and of trusting human relationships.

> **Improvisation is:**
>
> • thinking about what will move this situation forward, not blocking.
>
> • acting with intention towards what this moment needs, and moving towards your overall direction.
>
> • knowing fully that what you offer (or don't offer) impacts the well being of your team.
>
> • paying attention to everything in the moment so you can make your best offer.

Accepting/Blocking

Accepting and blocking[5] are terms that describe what happens to offers. An offer is accepted when one of the players responds in a way that incorporates the offer. For example, if Player A is on stage at the opening of a scene and Player B comes onto the stage and says, "So, how are you feeling? Let's take your blood pressure," the offer is that Player B is a doctor and Player A is now the patient. If Player A proceeds to answer, "Yes, doctor. Good to see you," the offer has been accepted. If, on the other hand, Player A says, "Actually, I feel great. And I am at the grocery store," then the offer has been blocked, or not accepted.

> **We block when we:**
>
> • say "no."
>
> • fail to listen.
>
> • have a better idea.
>
> • change the subject.
>
> • tend to other tasks.
>
> • ignore the situation.
>
> • correct the speaker.
>
> • send disruptive body language.

Yes, and…

This tenet takes accepting an offer and does it one better. In the case of "Yes, and…," the offer is accepted and then moved forward in some way, by adding an offer, which in turn can be accepted and used by the other players. To build on our example above, to illustrate a "Yes, and…," Player A could have responded to the 'doctor' with a litany of health concerns, at once reinforcing her role as patient and giving the doctor much to choose from for his response. This tenet has been identified as a "mainstay of improv."[9]

In the Moment — Improv Style

While there is a great deal of spontaneity and 'unscriptedness' at the heart of improvisation, being 'in the moment' means a different set of things to improvisers. Players are not encouraged to do whatever they want in the moment, but to "use the present moment efficiently,"[15] which means recalling all the offers that have come before and "[m]aking patterns and connection."[4] Improvisers are not just in the moment, but in all the moments. By this I mean, good players use everything that has been offered before as possible fodder. Careful listening, a good memory, and close observation skills are fostered, practiced, and appreciated among players.

Team Scene/Do Not Play-Write

One of the overarching understandings within improv troupes is the collective creation of scenes. No one person is responsible for the scene. Good improv troupes know that together is better. They take or assume collective accountability for the scene's unfolding; each player has the "right and responsibility to move the scene forward."[15]

Be a Good Player

With this focus on troupe dynamics and collective creation, being a good player matters. Many of these rules are shared as part of "the etiquette of ensemble,"[27] and one of the key ways a player is considered a 'good' troupe member is by taking care of the other members.[4, 19] In improv terms, this is done in a number of ways. A player should work to build trust, which is done by accepting and building on offers.[10, 15] Players should strive to make each other look good, which is done by noticing connections and by using all offers so there can be no mistakes.[4, 10, 19]

Be Comfortable with Possibility

To be successful with improvisation, one must realize that possibilities abound. That bowl in a player's hand can transform into a hat, a shield, or a UFO — all at a moment's notice. Of all the possibilities a player can choose from, one will stand out based on past experience, current interest, curiosity, playfulness, or possibility because of the relationship the player has with the person who made the offer. And the other players need to be ready to accept what is offered.

The Making of an Ensemble

> Take for example a teacher who tries a new song at circle time and it flops. This can be handled any number of ways. A co-teacher could say, "Yeah, that really didn't seem to work" and walk away. Or, the co-teacher could find something in that offer (of trying something new to respond to and accept) by saying, "I noticed you tried a new song today; adding new language to the kids' morning is such a plus."

An ensemble, the coming-together of a group, is a key element in improvisational troupes. It is what makes a troupe, a troupe. Being an ensemble involves a sense of trust, which includes knowing that troupemates will take care of each other. This taking care provides the comfort to take risks, because members know that regardless of what happens, the other members will find a way to be supportive.

Notice, the co-teacher found something to accept (the new vocabulary) in what the teacher offered. To turn it into a "yes, and..." the co-teacher might add, "That inspired me to find some new books to bring in." The magic in these small moments is built upon by recognizing that something valuable was offered. The "yes, and…" the co-teacher offered, further validated the teacher's purpose, made it explicit, and built on it.

In this setting, trust, risk, and comfort become intertwined. Relationships are strengthened when members pay attention to these moments together. The ensemble is built through active collaboration. As members trust each other and build a relationship, they go on to actively create together. This collaboration, in turn, strengthens the dispositions to take risks and to trust, which further builds the relationship. A positive feedback loop is created. The foundation of trusting oneself, trusting children, and trusting the moment becomes the norm.

It is as if this strategy of supporting improvisational dispositions composes a meta-set of skills transferable across content domains. In reviewing Moshavi's research[18] focusing on benefits to managerial students who practiced improvisational tenets,

- ■ we see gains in: "interpersonal communication, problem solving, team building, developing trust, enhancing creativity and innovation, reducing risk/fear of failure, adaptability" (p. 441).

- ■ success was not right answers given and/or wrong answers avoided, but "success is based on all classmates sharing responsibility for the outcome" (p. 444).

- ■ practice focused on "empowering them to help their classmates" (p. 444).

This is incredibly powerful and transformative. In Moshavi's list of skills I see desired outcomes in excellent child care programming. In addition, adults who model vibrancy in their interactions can mirror back to children "rich and complex possible selves who are disposed to improvise, innovate, and critique."[1]

What makes the difference between ideas getting accepted and those that are blocked? Sometimes it is the idea itself and sometimes it is about the dispo-

sition of the person receiving the idea. Each of us can probably call to mind a person who seems to block any idea from going forward. Whether calling on the budget, the weather, or anything in-between, "no" seems to be the first word out of their mouths.

During a staff meeting, a teacher suggests that your program have a summer barbecue with a pig roast; you know that the newest enrolled family is vegetarian. What do you say?

One option would be to shut down the idea because it isn't inclusive. In this case, it's clear that accepting the whole offer as it stands would cause some discomfort for a family. But, if this program practices finding **something** in the offer to accept, the assistant director might say, "I really like your inclination to share hospitality with everyone." In that way, she isn't accepting the premise of the pig roast, but she is finding a way to say "yes" and keep the conversation moving forward towards a shared goal of family engagement. The next steps of conversation could include finding a menu plan that would work for all families.

Keep improv as a focus by:

- expecting continuous change and challenge.

- being willing to take risks and make mistakes.

- seeking collaboration and peer support.

- valuing our own play as well as the children's.

- taking delight in development: the children's, our own, and the development of a situation as a whole.

But that isn't the only way we block people's ideas. Blocking can be subtle, a shift in eye contact, or a folding of the arms over the chest. Blocking can be dangerous because it has a chilling effect on staff offering their best ideas and best work. In every proposal, there is usually something that can be identified as worthy of pursuing or exploring further. For example, take this scenario in a typical child care program.

Imagine a staff person storms in, upset and yelling because someone didn't come back from break on time and now the afternoon schedule has been compromised. While it isn't appropriate to encourage anyone speaking badly about colleagues, it is okay to find something in this conversation to say "yes" to and further collaborate: "I can really appreciate how much you care that this impacts our afternoon schedule so much." Even in that upset, there is a kernel that can be held onto and moved forward.

Accepting offers does not mean that you take whatever someone says and run with it. It means that somehow you locate some piece of what was said as a possibility to explore further. Even with big emotions, this practice can be helpful.

Madson reminds us, "The 'yes' invites us to find out what is right about the situation, what is good about the offer, and what is worthy in the proposal" (p. 32).[15]

The searching for the "yes" can be classified as a kind of responsiveness. Responsiveness does not mean moving willy-nilly through each moment 'responding' to whatever comes up and reacting to it. Responsiveness takes into consideration what has gone before, what is known about the person and context, and is thoughtful. This responsiveness can be pres-

ent in several forms: listening, tailoring interactions, and a colleague's 'presence' — both in physical and mental ways. And finally, this responsiveness and intentional disposition captures something in the humanity of our work as well: "the practice of improvisation teaches something that we are hungry to understand: how to be in harmony with one another and how to have fun" (Madson, 2005, p. 20).

References

1. Carr, M., & Lee, W. (2012). *Learning stories: Constructing learner identities in early education.* London: SAGE Publications.

2. DeZutter, S. (2011). "Professional improvisation and teacher education: Opening the conversation." In R. K. Sawyer (Ed.) (2011), *Structure and improvisation in creative teaching* (pp. 27-50). Cambridge: Cambridge University Press.

3. Hackbert, P. H. (2011). "Using improvisational exercises in general education to advance creativity, inventiveness, and innovation." *U.S. China Education Review, 7*(10), 10- 21.

4. Halpern, C., Close, D., & Johnson, K. (1994). *Truth in comedy: The manual of improvisation.* Colorado Springs, CO: Meriwether Publishing Ltd.

5. Johnstone, K. (1979). *Impro: Improvisation and the theatre.* London: Methuen Publishing Limited.

6. Katz, L. & Raths, J. (1985). "Dispositions as goals for teacher education." *Teaching and Teacher Education, 1*(4), 301-307.

7. Lobman, C. (1993). "The bugs are coming!: Improvisation and early childhood teaching." *Young Children, 58*(3), 18- 23.

8. Lobman, C. (2003). "What should we create today?: Improvisational teaching in play-based classrooms." *Early Years: An International Journal of Research and Development, 23*(2), 131-142.

9. Lobman, C. (2005). "'Yes, and…': The uses of improvisation for early childhood professional development." *Journal of Early Childhood Teacher Education, 26*(3), 305-319.

10. Lobman, C. (2006). "Improvisation: An analytic tool for examining teacher-child interactions in the early childhood classroom." *Early Childhood Research Quarterly, 21,* 455-470.

11. Lobman, C. (2011). "Improvising within the system: Creating new teacher performances in inner-city schools." In R. K. Sawyer (Ed.) (2011), *Structure and improvisation in creative teaching* (pp. 73-93). Cambridge: Cambridge University Press.

12. Lobman, C., & Lundquist, M. (2007). *Unscripted learning: Using improv activities across the K-8 curriculum.* New York: Teachers College Press.

13. Lobman, C., & Ryan, S. (2008). "Creating an effective system of early childhood teacher education and professional development: Conversations with Stakeholders." *Educational Policy, 22*(4), 515-540.

14. Lobman, C., & Ryan, S. (2007). "Differing discourses on early childhood teacher development" *Journal of Early Childhood Teacher Education, 28*(4), 367-380.

15. Madson, P. R. (2005). *Improv wisdom: Don't prepare, just show up.* New York: Bell Tower.

16. Miller, D. (2008). *Teaching with intention: Defining beliefs, aligning practice, taking action.* Markham/Portland: Pembroke Publishers/Stenhouse Publishers.

17. Miller, B. C. (2003). *Quick team-building activities for busy managers: 50 exercises that get results in just 15 minutes.* New York: AMACOM.

18. Moshavi, D. (2001). "'Yes, and...': Introducing improvisational theatre techniques to the management classroom." *Journal of Management Education, 25*(4), 437-449.

19. Salinsky, T., & Frances-White, D. (2008). *The improv handbook: The ultimate guide to improvising in comedy, theatre, and beyond.* New York: Continuum.

20. Sawyer, R. K. (2011a). "What makes good teachers great?: The artful balance of structure and improvisation." In R. K. Sawyer (Ed.) (2011), *Structure and improvisation in creative teaching* (pp. 1-24). Cambridge: Cambridge University Press.

21. Sawyer, R. K. (Ed.) (2011b). *Structure and improvisation in creative teaching.* Cambridge: Cambridge University Press.

22. Sawyer, R. K. (2006). "Educating for innovation." *Thinking skills and creativity, 1,* 41-48.

23. Sawyer, R. K. (2004a). "Creative teaching: Collaborative discussion as disciplined improvisation." *Educational Researcher, 33*(2), 12-20.

24. Sawyer, R. K. (2004b). "Improvised lessons: Collaborative discussion in the constructivist classroom." *Teaching Education, 15*(2), 189-201.

25. Sawyer, R. K. (2003). *Improvised dialogues: Emergence and creativity in conversation.* Westport, CT: Greenwood.

26. Sawyer, R. K. (1997). *Pretend play as improvisation: Conversation in the preschool classroom.* Mahwah, NJ: Erlbaum.

27. Smith, K., & McKnight, K. S. (2009). "Remembering to laugh and explore: Improvisational activities for literacy teaching in urban classrooms." *International Journal of Education & the Arts, 10*(12). Retrieved 9/18/12 from www.ijea.org/v10n12/

28. Whitaker, T., & Breaux, A. (2013). *The ten-minute inservice: 40 quick training sessions that build teacher effectiveness.* San Francisco: Jossey-Bass.

Kelly Matthews

Kelly Matthews, owner of A Place for You Consulting in Oshkosh, Wisconsin, loves the playful mindfulness of improvisation, promotes experiential learning, and adores combining these two passions in her innovative offerings of professional development around the country. She can be reached at APlaceForYouConsult@yahoo.com.

Learning to Play Well with Others

And Other Lessons in Leadership I've Learned Along the Way

by Jeny Searcy

Many years ago someone I respected said to me, "If you were to get a kindergarten report card, it would say 'Jeny does not play well with others.'" The statement was made to show why, in this person's assessment, I could never be a good manager or leader; I was simply too independent and unconcerned about others' input. Because I respected and trusted this person, I accepted the statement and busied myself in finding support work where I never had to be in charge. After all, I did not 'play well with others.'

For several years after college, I looked for and did quite well in secondary administrative positions. My attitude was "give me a task and then just get out of my way — I'll take care of it." It worked, both for me and for employers. Then — almost by accident — I entered the field of Early Childhood Education and started on a leadership journey — a journey of many steps. And with those steps, I learned some important lessons.

Creating Partnerships

My first job in Early Childhood was as Center Director/Teacher in a new Head Start Center in Tipton, Oklahoma. I was lead teacher for 20 four year olds and the 'boss' of a staff of three.

Although I knew nothing at all about young children (except my own two, who were then starting public school) or management, I plunged in. Fear and uncertainty led me to a basic principle of good leadership; I worked to make my staff and me into a team. In her book *A Great Place to Work*, Paula Jorde Bloom (1997) emphasizes the value of shared decision making and joint management. What the literature shows, we at Tipton Head Start managed to do instinctively (or through sheer terror at making a mistake!). We were partners and we worked toward a common vision — giving our four year olds the best possible program. Playwright Henrick Ibsen wrote, "A community is like a ship; everyone has to be prepared to take the helm," and I journeyed toward leadership on this ship.

Lesson Learned: Trust your instincts. Whether you are a new or seasoned director, there are some things that are just going to 'feel' right. Be attuned to your feelings and trust them.

Meeting Needs and Expanding Horizons

Abraham Maslow's hierarchy of human needs begins with essential physical/body needs. Then come the "essential safety, security, protection needs."

I responded to this instinctively, too. I often said, "If all I can do is keep these kids safe and warm and cared for four hours a day and make sure they have something nourishing to eat, I have accomplished something important." And I still believe that. I wanted to go beyond that, though, and give children new experiences. Working with children from low-income families in a rural Oklahoma town (population 1,117), opportunities were limited. We found ways, however, to expand. We introduced a reading program, we took kids on a rotating basis to the library, and we took field trips. We went to the ballet, to plays, and to concerts. We had visitors come into the center to sing, read, and perform. I could have kept the kids safe and warm in the center and no one would have thought any less of me and the center, but I would have thought less of myself. And so, by pushing, expanding, and caring about the kids, I took another step on my journey.

Lesson Learned: Use community resources. Whether you work in Tipton or Tulsa, there are people 'out there' who are willing to come to your program and perform, teach, and share. It can be a professional troupe, a college student, or even the neighbor who whistles. It can take some work to find these people, but the efforts are worth it.

Seeing the Needs of the Individuals

After several years, I went to work as a Literacy Specialist with another agency's Head Start program. As Literacy Specialist, my role was to train, mentor, and monitor the classroom teachers in expanding literacy in the Head Start classrooms. I coordinated a series of training workshops for the lead teachers in the classrooms — one session per month to examine one of the sections of literacy for preschool children (reading aloud, pre-writing, language development). The teachers, from a three county area, came to my site. We had a great time, and the ideas I shared with them were evident in their classrooms.

The next school year, however, I started the same program with the teacher assistants/aides. This did not work as well. The teacher assistants/aides didn't seem as interested, and I felt as if I was getting nowhere. So I modified the program and traveled to each site once a month. There I could sit down with just the two or three teacher assistants and talk about literacy and create lessons about how their practices affected them and the children in their classrooms. It may have been my 'big picture' approach that was difficult for these teacher assistants/aides to see; perhaps they felt powerless to effect change in their classrooms. Whatever the reason, when I spent one-on-one time with them, they accepted my help. A powerful step in leadership for me: a good leader must recognize that, even when an organization has a common goal, the methods for reaching that goal can be and should be as varied as the individuals who work to achieve it.

Lesson Learned: We learn in early childhood classes that each child has his or her own learning style and that we should respect that. Remember that for your staff as well. Some will speak up at staff meetings; others will not. Some like lecture-type training; others relate better to hands-on. Whatever the need or style of the staff members, learn it and provide for it.

Seeing beyond Problems and Setting Common Goals

In 2006 I was hired to be the Director of Sunbeam Child Development Center. Sunbeam serves 48 children between the ages of birth and five in two Early Head Start classrooms, one three-year-old classroom, and one pre-kindergarten classroom. It has a staff of 13 people. Somehow I thought I was competent to handle all of this. The first six months were beyond description. Staff members quit, the public school took three months to supply a teacher for the pre-kindergarten classroom, and there were two federal reviews. The center had always boasted that it accepted children who had been asked to leave other centers, and we had a lot of children with behavior problems. I worked from open to close

(6:30 am to 5:30 pm) every day and cried, either on my way to work or on my way home — sometimes both.

Gradually, however, things began to change. As staff members quit, I was able to replace them with people who had the same goals that I had and who could complement my strengths and support my weaknesses. When the public school teacher finally came, we were able to set goals for her classroom together. We passed reviews with flying colors. And while the children's behavior didn't improve overnight, I began to see the children as individuals and not just as problems to be fixed.

Lesson Learned: Some things just take time. As hard as it is for most of us to accept, most problems can't be fixed immediately. Take some time, cry a little, and hang on. It will get better.

Accepting Support: Letting Go, Delegating, and Trusting

At Sunbeam, I made it my goal to not only function as the 'director,' but to be willing to do whatever the staff had to do. I substituted in the classrooms, I cooked, I fixed toilets, and I planned programs. I kept an open-door policy so that the staff members and parents could visit at any time. I felt that I had to prove I was a member of the team. After six months, I was nominated by all 13 members of the CDC staff as Sunbeam's Employee of the Month. I thought I had truly arrived as a leader! After all, Roger Neugebauer wrote in *Exchange*, "The good director doesn't make people love her, but makes people love to work for her." I had accomplished that, hadn't I? I was good — or was I?

Then I attended a leadership class conducted by author Linda Dowling who had written *Mentor Manager/Mentor Parent: How to Develop Responsible People and Build Successful Relationships at Work and at Home* (Dowling & Mielenz, 2002). I thought I was on safe ground here. I believed I had proved I was a

mentor leader. After all, my staff liked me and I never asked them to do anything that I wasn't willing to do myself. When I shared this with Ms. Dowling, she replied, "Jeny, you aren't being a mentor to your staff; you're being a martyr."

Whoa! All my good ideas and hard work weren't the right thing? Maybe I needed to stand back a little. At about the same time, I learned the following phrase: "Good supervision is not what happens when you are there; it is what happens when you are NOT there." Maybe my being there for the staff at all times was allowing them to *lean* and NOT allowing them to *learn*. Maybe I should step back and trust the staff. If I have hired the right people, they don't need me to do everything for them. As General George S. Patton said, "Don't tell people how to do things. Tell them what to do and let them surprise you with the results."

Lesson Learned: Respect and listen to your staff. Currently, I do one-on-one protected reflection time with each staff member for 45 minutes each month. I love listening to the teachers' ideas, their worries, and their joys — and the children, the teachers, and I all benefit.

Embracing Lifelong Learning

After I completed my first year as director, I was accepted into the Oklahoma Center for Early Childhood Professional Development's (CECPD's) Leadership Academy. One day a month for five months, I attended leadership classes. The topics ranged from communication and trust to mentoring and advocacy. In a group of peers (other directors from around Oklahoma), we developed our leadership skills. For the very first time, I was actually getting leadership training! I received some wonderful books (see Resources). Through the leadership academy, I learned that there were people out there and that it was safe and helpful to network with peers.

In the midst of the Leadership Academy, I started work on my Master's degree at the University of

Central Oklahoma. The theme of my first class? Leadership! As we worked our way through theories, I became more and more convinced of several principles:

- Leaders are made, not born.

- Leaders have to get on the level of those around them, not lead from above.

- Leaders have to be flexible.

- Leadership is a journey, not a destination.

To be an effective leader, I must continue to grow and be willing to change. There is not one 'leadership style,' one method of leadership that is successful in any situation. I must continue to grow, to change, and to learn. Rosabeth Moss Kantor, a professor of leadership and management at Harvard University wrote, "Leaders are more powerful role models when they learn than when they teach."

Lesson Learned: Never, ever stop learning or think you know it all. If you aren't willing to learn, to change, and to stretch your thinking, you wither. Go to classes, read books, talk to peers and mentors — constantly be open to opportunities to learn.

Conclusion

I expect that my journey will continue. I see myself moving from someone who didn't 'play well with others' to someone who is a good playmate. Throughout the journey, regardless of its length, there is one essential lesson for leaders in our field: *Find joy in the journey.* Whether it is dancing with the toddlers or sharing a teacher's excitement developing a new activity, take time to savor the moments. Despite the stress, the tears, and the pressure, there is truly joy in the journey.

References

Bloom, P. J. (1988). *A great place to work: Improving conditions for staff in young children's programs.* Washington, DC: NAEYC.

Dowling, L., & Mielenz, C. C. (2002). *Mentor manager/mentor parent: How to develop responsible people and build successful relationships at work and at home.* Austin, TX: TurnKey Press.

Resources

Bloom, P. J. (2007). *From the inside out: The power of reflection and self-awareness.* Washington, DC: NAEYC.

Bloom, P. J. (2003). *Leadership in action: How effective directors get things done.* Lake Bluff, IL: New Horizons.

Neugebauer, B., & Neugebauer, R. (1998). *The art of leadership: Managing early childhood organizations.* Redmond, WA: Exchange Press.

Jeny Searcy

With a degree in secondary speech education, Jeny Searcy rather unexpectedly entered the field of early childhood education in the early 1990s, when she became Director/Teacher of the Head Start Center in Tipton, Oklahoma. Since then she has worked as a Disability Specialist, Mental Health Specialist, and Literacy Specialist with Southwest Community Action Group. After a lifetime in rural southwest Oklahoma, Jeny moved to Oklahoma City in 2004. In 2006, she became Director of the Sunbeam Child Development Center. She recently began work on her Master's Degree in Early Childhood Education. In the fall of 2008, Jeny became supervisor of the Teachers of Infants, Toddlers, and Twos at The Children's Place at INTEGRIS Baptist Medical Center in Oklahoma City. Jeny is married with two grown children. In the past year, her family has grown to include one daughter-in-law, one son-in-law, and one grandson Geoffrey — the most perfect baby in the world!

Indicators of Effective Teamwork

by Margie Carter

In the past few months I've received a number of calls from directors and teachers asking for help with team building on their staff. The problems they describe vary from site to site: a Head Start teacher with a decade and a half of experience finds she can't work with her new assistant; a director of a child care program is concerned that some staff are highly involved in decision-making, while others under participate and don't lend their voice or time; another director worries about constant bickering among her teachers over what seem like petty issues; a Reggio-inspired program is struggling to understand what the Italians really mean by this concept of collaboration among teachers, children, and families.

The language of teamwork and collaboration is taken for granted in our professional discourse, but walking the talk is quite another thing. These accomplishments require time to build relationships, an ability to take multiple perspectives, and a willingness to hang in there when tensions escalate. The typical child care setting has difficulty providing time for meaningful adult interactions away from the children. Directors and other program supervisors have many demands on their attention and find it difficult to be proactive in building a cohesive team. Many lack the experience to know how to specifically nurture the dispositions and mentor the skills of being a collaborator and team player.

Beyond the nice gestures of birthday acknowledgments and creating a secret pals activity, directors often overlook the importance of team-building work until faced with a significant problem. Then the task becomes remediation, akin to weeding a garden that has gotten out of control, rather than a thoughtful plan of fertilizing and cultivating harmonious growth.

Working with programs to build strong teams and the ability to collaborate, I focus on recognizing key indicators that can be found in a program. Getting each person to identify what they look for in each of these areas begins an important dialogue where mutual understanding and accountability can be shaped.

Clear Communications

It goes without saying that people have different communication styles and skills, but these often go unacknowledged and become the source of growing tension on a staff. Part of our new staff orientation and ongoing development work needs to include guidelines for effective communications and clarity on the communication systems and policies of the program.

Strategy:
Develop, distribute, and role play communication guidelines

Take time in a staff meeting or retreat to brainstorm and develop written guidelines on what people want from each other in the way of good communications. Make sure each person states his view and that concepts such as listening, talking, writing, and body language are discussed. Choose the ideas that everyone agrees on to begin your list and then negotiate what to write for areas where there are different views. Remember to include something about how you want communication channels or protocol to work in your program.

To be sure everyone understands and agrees, develop some short role plays for people to practice using the guidelines. As you debrief the role play, review your written guidelines to see if they need more clarity. If your role plays reveal that staff need more communication skills, build that into your staff development plans.

Distribute, post, and periodically revisit your communication guidelines and make sure they become part of your new staff orientation packet and are referenced in your annual staff evaluation process.

Respectful Interactions and Demonstrations of Trust

Respect and trust are words easily thrown about in conversations, but what do they look like in the day-to-day life of a child care program? Taking the time to identify the attitudinal and behavioral aspects of respect and trust is a wise investment of your precious staff meeting time.

Strategy:
Identify the elements of respect and trust

Using a process similar to the one described above, devote some of your staff development hours to getting everyone 's views on what respect and trust specifically look like in given situations. To launch the discussion, ask people to first read and finish the following sentences with their own ideas:

A person who shows me respect is thoughtful about…

A person I give respect to knows how to…

I feel trusted by someone when she or he…

I will trust someone after she or he…

From the ideas generated, make a list of specific behaviors that generate trust and respect. Then present several short scenarios of typical encounters in a program where trust and respect can become an issue (i.e., arriving late to work, sharing personal information, giving a criticism, asking for help, or taking a different approach than your co-workers).

Divide into two groups with one developing a list of things that a staff member could do that would erode the possibility of trust or respect in this situation, while the other group identifies actions that could build trust. As a whole group, compare your lists to give staff a mirror on how their own ideas might play themselves out in real situations. Review your beginning list one more time for any additions or changes before it gets written and posted as a reference point for future interactions.

Using Conflicts to Discover and Negotiate Different Perspectives

Whenever a group of people comes together, especially with the conscious intent of influencing a group of children, the personal and professional growth available to them is enormous. This benefit of the work is worth stressing again and again, especially as you enter areas of conflict. Having some initial practice in consciously naming and working with different viewpoints establishes a foundation before the going gets rough.

In many early childhood programs, there are policies and practices that are taken for granted with little discussion or questioning. Someone in the past may have set these up according to a personal preference, or the policies may have been adopted from professional definitions of best practices. In any case, it is useful to periodically explore the assumptions underlying certain practices so that everyone is clear about why the program has specific policies. A chance to discuss these issues also provides an opportunity to identify and negotiate any conflicts of values among staff, and possibly between a teacher and parent.

Strategy:
Explore different values

Teachers and caregivers benefit from the opportunity to examine and name the influences on their own values and preferred practices. A simple way to do this in a staff meeting is to write on separate pieces of paper possible opposing viewpoints on policies and then post them around the room Ask everyone to find one viewpoint they wish to discuss, go to that paper, and talk with others there. They don't have to agree with the viewpoint, but they should at least have strong sentiments that they would like to discuss. Things you write on these papers could include:

■ Children should primarily be allowed to make choices and negotiate with adults.

■ Children should primarily be offered limited choices and non-negotiable guidelines from adults.

■ Children should call adults by their first names.

■ Children should address adults by Mr. or Ms. or Teacher with her or his name.

■ Children should be separated from the group or put in time-out when they don't follow the rules.

■ Children should be redirected and involved in other activities when they don't follow the rules.

■ Children should be required to try at least one bite of all the food served.

■ Children should be allowed to follow their own food preferences when eating.

■ Children should be allowed to get messy and dirty when they play in our program.

■ Children should be guided to keep their hair and clothes clean when they play in our program.

Some of these statements reflect or contradict prevailing views in our professional literature. This is a good place to acknowledge that our standards have been primarily shaped through a white middle-class lens. We need to open the dialogue and negotiate conflicting beliefs.

In the debriefing discussion ask whether people found similarities or differences with others in their group. Were they there because they agreed or disagreed with the viewpoint? When teachers are asked to carry out practices different from their own belief systems, the situation is ripe for resentment and subversion. On the other hand, when you create a climate to discover and negotiate different perspectives, you can often avoid the good guy/bad guy mentality and develop acceptable compromises.

Strategy:
Play with different communication styles

Sometimes people make judgments about each other based on differences in communication styles. This could be a personal or cultural issue, but in either circumstance, it's useful to understand what's happening. Here's a playful way to explore how we send and receive information and feelings.

Ask your staff to consider possible labels for acceptable communication styles and then choose four or five to work with. The term 'acceptable' is a subjective one. Our intent here is to avoid negative labels such as caustic, attacking, manipulative, or defensive, and identify a variety of other styles that have a useful place in communicating. For instance, friendly, humorous, creative, decisive, analytical direct or indirect could be selected as styles for exploration.

Spend a minute defining what is meant by each of these styles. Then divide the large group into as many small groups as there are styles, and assign one style to each small group. Ask each group to generate a list of common phrases that you might hear someone from that style use. For example, the lists might look something like this:

Friendly Style:

- You have great ideas.

- I like what you said.

- They might not like that.

Creative Style:

- Anything is possible.

- Let's keep brainstorming.

- What if we flipped that around?

Decisive Style:

- Let's not waste time.

- We have to decide one way or another.

- I want to know what we're going to do.

Analytical Style:

- I think we should do a survey.

- The facts speak for themselves.

- We need more evidence.

Once you've given each group the time to come up with a list of three or four phrases, ask for a volunteer from each group and conduct a communications role-play. Choose a topic that isn't emotionally loaded for the volunteers to discuss. An example might be what color the center should paint its walls, what kinds of plants to get for the lounge, or what software should be purchased for your computers. As you facilitate the brief discussion, ask each volunteer to try to use as many of the phrases on their list as possible in the situation. Along with being able to laugh and get a new perspective on how style might look in a group setting, you can debrief this activity to explore the strengths and weaknesses of each style and the barriers that can occur when we judge a person's contribution by their communication style. Staff members might enjoy identifying their own style and exploring how it can potentially conflict with another.

Building on Each Other's Ideas and Strengths

As with children, adults need coaching on how to participate in collaborative thinking and work projects. It doesn't come automatically. Activities such as the above can help identify the strengths that each person's style brings to the process. These should be named and celebrated. From there you can practice finding ways to get everyone's perspective, experience, and skills acknowledged and involved.

Strategy:
Pass the paper to build on ideas

Whatever the topic, you can divide your staff into small groups so that there is more time for everyone to offer their ideas during your staff meetings. Give each group an identical piece of chart paper, divided into three columns. If the topic is an anti-bias issue, a child guidance issue, health and safety, or a parent concern, label the three columns: Issues Identified, Immediate Response, and Further Plans.

Give each group a scenario related to the topic to discuss and write out their responses to the first column. After some time, have them pass their papers and scenario to the next group and, after reading what the previous group wrote in the first column, begin working on the second. Pass the paper and repeat this process for the third column. Then give each group their original paper to get the benefit of all the other groups' thinking and consider additional perspectives.

Reliability and Responsibility

You can be a thoughtful, sensitive person with terrific ideas, but if you don't show up on time for work, forget to fill out your paperwork, or neglect to make that critical call to a parent, you can hardly be called a team player. Reliability and responsibility are the ultimate behaviors that indicate whether clear communications, respect, trust, negotiating different perspectives and building on each other's strengths are alive and well and reflecting effective team work in your program.

Margie Carter

Margie Carter is the co-founder of Harvest Resources Associates (www.ecetrainers.com) and the co-author of numerous books and early childhood videos. As she moves towards retirement years, her professional work is focused on highlighting and supporting the inspiring work of new leaders and uplifting the voices and leadership of teachers in the field.

When Friction Flares

Dealing with Staff Conflict

by Roger Neugebauer

"Aside from the harm an uncontrolled conflict does to an organization, your inability as manager to control it may lead to your overthrow, either by angry contestants or by impatient bystanders."
Theodore Caplow

"Your job in resolving personality conflicts between your subordinates is to make the person involved in the conflict aware [of] how his or her behavior is adversely affecting others, and how it is thereby adversely affecting the operation."
Thomas L. Quick

These are the times that try directors' souls — when arguments erupt over the cleanup of shared space, when staff meetings turn into acrimonious debates over lousy working conditions, when two teachers every day find new pretexts to prolong their personal feud.

Wouldn't it be wonderful if you could wave a magic wand and all this disharmony would disappear? Unfortunately, in a demanding, interaction-intensive profession such as early childhood education, where pressures and feelings run high, conflict is inevitable.

There is no way a director can, or even should, drive all conflict out. The challenge is how to manage dissension so that it contributes to the growth, and not the deterioration, of the organization. The following are some guidelines for accomplishing this.

Encourage Healthy Conflict

Asking a center director to foster conflict may seem counterproductive. However, in a creative organization, the clash of ideas and opinions keeps the organization growing and improving. In a creative organization, the types of healthy conflict described in the "Signs of Healthy Conflict" box happen all the time.

As a leader in your organization, there are a number of steps you can take to promote healthy conflict:

• Don't let your ego run amok

I recently participated on a committee of teachers and board members tussling with the growing need for infant care. For months we hotly debated whether the center should offer infant care, where we could locate it, and how much we would have to charge to provide a high-quality program. When we presented our recommendations to the full board, a lively discussion ensued. Finally, the director took the floor and stated that she didn't believe children that young should be in a center. After her statement, the

Signs of Healthy Conflict

Conflict among staff in a center can be constructive if it...

- generates new ideas, new perspectives.

- provokes an evaluation of organizational structures or center design.

- brings individuals' reservations and objections out into the open.

- heightens the debate about pending decisions or problems.

- forces the reexamination of current goals, policies, or practices.

- focuses attention on problems inhibiting performance at the center.

- energizes staff — gets them actively involved in the life of the center.

discussion sort of petered out until finally a motion was made and passed to table the recommendations indefinitely.

This director had no intention of throwing a wet blanket on the debate — she assumed she simply was expressing her views as one member of the board. What she failed to take into account was that the opinion of the leader of any organization is packed with positional power. As a leader, unless you work hard to undermine your authority by behaving like a fool, your opinions may exert an overwhelming influence on discussions.

If you want your staff to express their opinions, be it in meetings or in one-to-one discussions, you must exercise discretion in expressing your own opinions. This is not easy.

Most directors I have met over the years tend to be take-charge people. They care deeply about the success of their centers and take it personally when things go wrong. Their egos are heavily invested in their work, and they like to have things done their way.

Take-charge directors often do unintentionally put a damper on the clash of ideas in their centers by jumping in with a position on every issue. Particularly if a director has strong verbal skills, she can easily dominate any discussion. If you value the expertise and insights of your staff members, you need to keep your ego in check. Resist that very natural urge to voice your opinion on anything and everything — at least until everyone else has had their say.

• Beware the peacemaker

Often within families there is an unspoken rule that one should not express angry feelings. On the surface this creates a placid appearance. But the result is that anger continues and festers, potentially causing long-term emotional difficulties for family members.

The same scenario can play itself out in organizations. When emotions erupt at the center, a peacemaker (maybe the director, maybe not) will rush in and urge everyone to calm down and keep their angry feelings in check. Once again, this may still the waters, but it often leaves conflicts unresolved. Suppressed anger can eat away at staff morale and, if allowed to intensify, can result in an even greater explosion later on.

A wiser, though often less pleasant, course for a director to take is to foster an environment where the true expression of emotions is tolerated. In the long run, this results in a better working climate because conflict can be brought out in the open where it can be dealt with and resolved.

On the other hand, you don't want to create a haven for hotheads and chronic complainers. You need to follow three basic rules in dealing with expressions of anger...

First, don't answer anger with anger. If you respond to anger in kind, emotions can quickly escalate out of control.

Second, listen. When a staff member is letting off steam, don't interrupt, argue, or explain. Let them get the feelings out of their system as much as possible before you intervene.

Third, ask questions. To move a discussion toward a constructive stage, ask specific questions to clarify the cause of the problem and then start the exploration of solutions.

• Don't take it personally

You want to create an atmosphere in your center where all staff members feel free to voice questions, concerns, and objections — where healthy conflict flourishes. You want your staff members to be confident that they can confront you openly over organizational issues and not worry that you will hold this against them.

You can, of course, tell people that you welcome their critical comments, and write them memos assuring them that this is true. But the bottom line is that people won't believe this until you demonstrate your tolerance in real life.

In part, this requires a significant sell job on yourself. You must believe that you and your center will benefit from the clash of ideas and opinions. When a debate flares over teaching practices, the use of common space, the center's ratios or other program issues, you must truly view this debate as an opportunity to improve the program. If you are not comfortable with conflict and criticism, your body language will surely send out warning signals to staff members that their comments are not being well received.

You can also demonstrate that you welcome open discussions by rewarding people who take risks by saying what they think. At the end of a heated, maybe even emotional, debate in a staff meeting,

acknowledge that the discussion may have put many participants under stress, that you appreciate everyone's honesty and openness, and that you believe that the program will be the better for having dealt with the issues at hand.

If individual staff members appear to be particularly upset by a confrontation, take pains to reassure them in private that you bear no grudge toward those who disagree with you. Thank them for expressing their views. Smile and behave normally towards them.

Discourage Unhealthy Conflict

Not all conflict is positive. A dispute over an organizational issue, which is ignored by the director, can deteriorate into acrimony and bring down staff morale. A personal feud, which erupts between two or more staff members, can distract participants from doing their jobs. One important challenge for any director is to distinguish between healthy and unhealthy conflict. When conflict exhibits manifestations such as those listed in the "Signs of Unhealthy Conflict" box, you need to intervene.

• Don't allow conflicts to escalate

Often it is tempting to ignore a minor flare up among staff members and hope that it will fade away. Sometimes this may work, but more often than not the 'hands off' approach backfires.

An outbreak of hostility can eat away at staff morale and productivity. The longer you allow it to rage out of control, the more likely your credibility as a leader will be undermined as well. You must act quickly to contain damaging conflict. It is especially helpful to intervene before a private feud has boiled over into a public feud. Once positions have been taken in public, it will be harder to get disputants to back down for fear of losing face.

• Be a mediator, not a judge

When faced with a conflict among staff members, you may quickly develop an opinion about who is

---

Signs of Unhealthy Conflict

Conflict among staff in a center can be destructive if…

- one person or faction is bound and determined to emerge victorious.

- focus of the debate changes, but the adversaries remain the same.

- discussion never moves from complaints to solutions.

- staff members start taking sides.

- parents or other outside parties get drawn into the debate.

- continuing acrimony starts to erode staff morale.

- dissension continues, even after a decision is hammered out.

- debate focuses on personalities, not issues.

---

right and who is wrong. Your temptation will be to end the dispute immediately by playing the role of the judge and declaring a winner. More often than not, you end up being the loser in this case, no matter how wise your decision. The winners believe they were right all along and, therefore, owe you no thanks; and the losers end up bitter because you made a stupid or biased decision.

You are better off in the long run to play the role of an impartial mediator working with both parties to hammer out a compromise that all can support. In this case, both parties feel they had a hand in shaping the outcome and will be more committed to making it work.

• Match your response to the severity of the conflict

In the case of a minor squabble between two or more staff members, you may find it sufficient to communicate to the individuals involved that you recognize that a problem exists and that you expect them to work out a resolution themselves. Give them a deadline; check back to make sure they followed through.

If the individuals can't work out their own problem, you may need to bring them together in your office and force them to confront the issues causing the conflict. Ask each individual to state her perception of the problem and then her suggestions for a solution. Your role is to lead them to agree on a solution.

In some cases, such a face-to-face thrashing out of the issues may work. When emotions are running high, however, a confrontation may actually escalate the conflict. When one angry staff member confronts another in your presence, this may cause both parties to intensify their feelings. In order to save face, they may harden their positions.

In this case, you may need to play more of the role of a third-party intermediary. Interview each party to the conflict in private and ask him to explain the facts of the dispute as he sees them. Then present to each disputant, in as objective a manner as possible, a description of the other party's perception of the problem. Take the opportunity to point out inconsistencies in either party's positions — they are much more likely to agree to a 'clarification of the facts' with you than with the other party. In some cases, this clarification process may be enough to end the dispute.

If not, ask each party to propose potential solutions. Find commonalities among the solutions and see if you can gain agreement on those points by proposing them to each disputant separately. If necessary, suggest solutions of your own. In any case, work step-by-step to an acceptable compromise.

• Focus on behavior, not personalities

Your job as a leader is to make the organization succeed. Your concern in any personal feud, therefore, should not be on trying to bring harmony to a relationship gone sour, but on preventing the conflict from interfering with the functioning of the organization.

As a caring person, your natural inclination will be to want everyone on your staff to be on friendly terms at all times. However, unless you are a trained psychologist, you are not likely to be successful in changing people's attitudes toward each other.

But in focusing on behavior patterns, you are more likely to have success. Point out to disputants how their behavior is hurting their own performance as well as interfering with the performance of others. Don't allow yourself to get caught up with their personal issues. Focus your attention and theirs on changing their detrimental behavior.

Conflict is as normal a part of the life of a child care center as Legos® and finger Jell-O. By being out front in dealing with conflict as it occurs, a director can create a positive force out of the daily clash of ideas, opinions, and personalities.

Resources

Caplow, T. (1983). *Managing an organization*. New York: Holt, Rinehart and Winston.

Quick, T. L. (1977). *Person to person managing*. New York: St. Martin's Press.

Roger Neugebauer

Roger Neugebauer is publisher of *Exchange Magazine* and a co-founder of the World Forum Foundation.

Ten Teamwork Terminators and Some Sure Cures

by Hawaii Directors Network attendees

Teamwork is one of those all-American concepts like motherhood, apple pie, and developmentally appropriate practice. No director should lead on without it.

How to be a team builder was the focus of an Exchange management retreat in Hawaii. Participating directors shared a wide range of experiences and insights at this retreat, and these form the basis of this article.

One interesting insight at the retreat was that, as much as a director may want her staff to function as a team, she may be the biggest stumbling block to making it happen. Participants identified 10 behaviors that directors may engage in that unwittingly undermine team performance, as well as some keys to making the team work.

Playing Favorites

Nothing sours team spirit more quickly than a perception that some team members enjoy a privileged status. If you consistently single out one or two teachers for praise, give them preferential treatment in scheduling, or tend to seek their input more than anyone else's, other staff members will feel more like outsiders than team members.

Tolerating Laxity

If one staff member frequently arrives late, fails to help with clean up, or is lax in attending to the children, and you let this misbehavior go unchallenged, other staff members will resent having to work harder. They will blame you for caving in and will be less inclined to work hard for the common good.

Cowering from Conflict

Teacher A lashes out at Teacher B and stomps out of the staff meeting. You continue as if nothing has happened. Afterwards you make small talk with the two teachers separately hoping to jolly them out of their angry moods. Efforts to maintain an outward appearance of harmony may ease tensions in the short run, but the hostility remains and may draw others into the conflict.

Fuzzy Roles

To the extent that there is confusion about roles and responsibilities, energy that could be directed toward working with children and parents will be consumed by anxiety and frustration. For teachers to feel secure and focused, they need to know exactly what is expected of them. They need to know what tasks they hold final responsibility for, what tasks they share responsibility for, and what decisions they must clear with someone in authority before going ahead.

Inconsistency

In January, the director announces to staff that building self-esteem is going to be the center's number one goal. In February, she holds a staff meeting in which she shares her excitement about implementing a new environmental awareness curriculum.

In March, she decides it's time that the center take a stand on violence in the lives of children. Such vacillation, whether it be over curriculum goals, operating practices, or personnel procedures, contributes to a sense of uncertainty among the staff and a loss of credibility for the leadership.

The Tyranny of Taboos

Teamwork tends to bring out the best in people, to motivate team members to work hard for the common good. The focus of the team is on uniting the talents of individual team members. Teamwork is promoted by focusing on achieving goals, not on obeying rules. Directors who attempt to direct staff by promulgating rules and by punishing misbehavior will not build team spirit.

Staff that is motivated by team spirit will focus their energies on accomplishing goals. Staff that is directed

by rules and admonitions will focus their energies on avoiding punishment.

Holding On to the Reins

Many early childhood leaders have a difficult time releasing the reins of authority. They want to have the final say on every decision. By tightly controlling every activity, a knowledgeable director may assure that everything is done right — but with a significant cost in terms of staff morale. Staff will get the message that they are not trusted. They will see themselves more as dispensable machine parts than as valued team members. The bottom line is: Just let go.

Fake Participation

Even more demoralizing than an authoritarian director is a director who goes through the motions of inviting staff participation in shaping decisions and then ignores staff input when the final decisions are made. More often than not such behavior is not intentional. A director may believe in the value of staff involvement and genuinely reach out for advice. However, when it comes to the final decision, he may be so locked into his own point of view that he can't understand or be influenced by conflicting views. But whether or not the behavior is deliberate, the impact on the staff will be the same. Staff will feel misled, frustrated, and angry — certainly not in the mood to work hard for the team.

The Hindering Hierarchy

To be an enthusiastic team player, you need to believe that your contribution makes a difference. You need to feel valued and respected. In an organization with a formal or informal hierarchy it is hard to develop team spirit among staff who perceive themselves to be on the bottom rung of the ladder.

Many centers have evolved into a quasi caste system whereby the administrators are viewed as the bosses,

Keys to Building a Successful Team

• Make team building a priority

Teamwork doesn't just happen. A staff will not naturally evolve from a collection of individuals into a well-oiled team. The leader needs to identify teamwork as a high priority, gain the support of staff for the idea, and develop a deliberate process for making it happen.

Built into this process will need to be: 1) an open assessment of the talents and interests of all team members; 2) the development of goals that all team members are committed to accomplishing; and 3) the organizing of tasks and responsibilities in such a way that the talents and interests of all team members are put to best use.

• Keep your finger on the pulse

Periodically the leader should encourage the staff to stop and take a look at how the team-building process is going. Initially you may want to use a simple instrument such as the "Twenty Questions about Team Spirit" that appears at the end of article (you have the permission of *Exchange* to reproduce this freely for internal use).

Ask staff members if they would agree to fill this out, and ask them to do so anonymously. Tabulate the results and share them, unedited, with the entire staff. Focus on the areas where good things are happening, and then talk about those areas where progress needs to be made.

Elicit from the group first what suggestions they might have, add in your thoughts, and then try as a group to arrive at some specific steps to make. (Note: If at this point you simply step in and say, "Okay, here is what needs to happen!," staff members may not be inclined to share the responsibility for results.)

Try to use the same form to measure progress every six months or so. Then as your team begins to jell, you should be able simply to hold open discussions periodically to air concerns and develop solutions.

• Make meetings meaningful

Staff meetings that are boring, unfocused, or unimaginative actually can sap team spirit. Who cares about being a part of a team that can't get excited or that isn't fun to be with?

Staff meetings are the connection points that enable teamwork to develop. They should be the hub of your deliberate team-building process.

To be successful, staff meetings must engage the interest and enthusiasm of all participants. They must provide a safe environment in which staff members can challenge basic assumptions, take risks, stretch their thinking, ask stupid questions, and share their feelings.

Establish ground rules for team-building staff meetings that provide everyone equal opportunity to be heard and all ideas to be open to question. Every meeting appoint a different staff person to be the process monitor to make sure in a kindly way that these ground rules are observed.

Make meetings unpredictable so that people come to meetings eager to see what will happen next. Move meetings around to different rooms, different locations. People are more open to new ideas if they come in expecting something new than if they come in turned off expecting the same old stuff.

the head teachers as the educators, and the teacher aides as the workers. In such a system, the workers will not feel valued or respected, and certainly will not be motivated to become team players. In addition, any feelings of superiority the educators possess will get in the way of their ability to participate with fervor in a team effort.

Lack of Recognition

Being part of a smoothly functioning team is a gratifying experience. Working together to try out new ideas, to solve problems, to help each other grow, and to achieve results can be invigorating and fun. However, sometimes, especially in the early, rocky stages of team building, these intrinsic rewards are not enough. Team members who feel their hard work and special contributions are not appreciated will eventually want off the team.

Twenty Questions about Team Spirit

An Exchange Center Evaluation Form

_____   1. I understand the curriculum goals of the center.

_____   2. I am in agreement with these goals.

_____   3. I am proud to be associated with this center.

_____   4. I have no fear about expressing my opinions and concerns at the center.

_____   5. When I have something to say, people here really listen.

_____   6. I am kept up-to-date on developments at the center.

_____   7. I find staff meetings to be informative and productive.

_____   8. I have a clear understanding of my role at the center.

_____   9. My full range of skills is tapped in my work at the center.

_____   10. When important decisions are made, I am consulted, and my opinions are taken seriously.

_____   11. When decisions are made, new policies announced, or new goals set, the director sees to it that they are implemented.

_____   12. When conflicts arise between adults in the center, the director moves quickly and effectively to resolve them.

_____   13. When other problems arise at the center, the director moves quickly and effectively to solve them.

_____   14. When dealing with a problem, the director involves the appropriate staff members in helping work out a solution.

_____   15. I believe that I am treated fairly as an employee.

_____   16. I have not observed anyone else being treated unfairly.

_____   17. I don't believe any employee is granted favored status.

_____   18. I enjoy a friendly relationship with other staff members.

_____   19. I receive support from other staff members when I need help.

_____   20. I consistently receive valuable feedback about my performance.

The most important step the organization could take to improve team spirit is…

I am eager for team spirit to improve at our center, and here is what I am willing to do to help…